FIX THE SYSTEM

REFORM THE CONSTITUTION

John Marshall Cogswell

CAMPAIGN CONSTITUTION PRESS
BUENA VISTA, COLORADO

First printing 2012

ISBN 978-0-9857360-0-2
LCCN 2012941382

**ATTENTION CORPORATIONS, UNIVERSITIES,
COLLEGES, AND PROFESSIONAL ORGANIZATIONS:**
Quantity discounts are available on bulk purchases of this book for educational,
gift purposes, or as premiums for increasing magazine subscriptions or
renewals. Special books or book excerpts can also be created to fit specific needs.
For information, please contact Campaign Constitution Press,
PO Box 1430, 15099 County Road 350, Buena Vista, CO 81211.

www.campaignconstitution.com

DEDICATION

To my father, John Cogswell, who taught
me the lessons of the Founding Fathers.

ACKNOWLEDGMENTS

I gratefully acknowledge the support of my wife, Ann, who tolerated many days of a dining room table covered with papers and books and who never gave me anything but encouragement. I give special thanks to my secretary, Rebecca Cooling, whose conscientious attitude and expertise with the computer allowed her to craft my thoughts in presentable and proper form. I also thank her sister, Suzanne Miller, and Susan Wolfe, also secretaries, who contributed to the effort with smiles on their faces but with enough mystery in their manner to suggest that air of resignation that says, "There he goes again."

I thank my niece, Ashley Auld-Sharpshair, who, with a minimum of instruction, developed the early mechanics of the website and the logo, and also Jamie Utendorf-Hagen, who gave us many artistic ideas for presenting our materials. Without VistaWorks right here in Buena Vista, and its Bryan Jordon and Samuel Danger Palpant, I could never have established the website this book is intended to replicate.

In a departure from modesty, I acknowledge myself for not having invited anyone to help me in this venture, believing it would lead to too many arguments and discourage me from completing what I have in mind. I have undoubtedly made mistakes because of this but am confident they will be corrected by others. The important thing is to put these ideas on the table for the public to discuss as it decides whether our system is broken and, if so, how it can be fixed.

John M. Cogswell
May 11, 2012

NOTE TO THE READER

In writing the proposed amendments and essays that you will find in this book, I have referred to the masculine gender for the sake of simplicity. By doing this, I have not intended to slight the female gender in any way and trust all who read the materials will interpret "he" and related terms as references to both men and women.

I have also repeated some verbiage and quotations to assist the reader.

CONTENTS

Part 1: Campaign Constitution

Part 2: Proposed Amendments

Part 3: Essays

*   *   *

Pictures:

The advocates of error
Foresee the glorious morn,
And hear in shrinking terror,
The watchword of reform:
It rings from hill and valley,
It breaks oppression's chain.
A thousand freemen rally,
And swell the mighty strain.

—N. T. Munroe, circa 1850

PREFACE

Most of us love our country. Why is this? Why do we love America? We love the story of the Pilgrims and, later, Paul Revere and the American Revolution. We love that our Founding Fathers, who wrote our Constitution, were so smart and well educated and gave us a Constitution that has protected so many of our freedoms. We love the great American spirit of equal justice, equal rights, and equal opportunity for a better life. We are saddened by the wars whose battlefields have killed so many innocent people. But we love that we won, that we remained secure in our freedoms, and that our citizens had the creative genius to invent and produce those things that have made us stronger than our enemies.

We know now that the love we have for all of these things had a beginning and a reason. Can we say what it is? Can we write it down? Can we explain it to our children? Do we explain it to our children?

I read Professor Paul Woodruff's *Reverence: Renewing a Forgotten Virtue* (2001), which quotes from Protagoras, a great pre-Socratic thinker:

> Whenever they gathered into groups [early human beings] would do wrong to each other because they did not yet have the knowledge of how to form society. As a result they would scatter again and perish. And so Zeus, fearing that our whole

species would be wiped out, sent Hermes to bring reverence and justice to human beings, in order that these two would adorn society and bind people together in friendship.—Protagoras, Plato's *Protagoras,* 322 c.[1]

Before reverence and justice were distributed, ancient cities were battlefields. Without reverence and justice today, our nation will become a battlefield. The challenge is to rekindle reverence and justice by restoring faith in the people and to replace our current politicians with statesmen who put freedom, reverence, justice, and the best interests of the whole country first and their ambitions last.

Today, we are engaged on a battlefield of ideas. It is a battlefield whose outcome is freedom or tyranny. Our elected representatives in Washington have allowed their love of power to displace their love of country and to diminish the wisdom of the people. Our interests are not being protected. The result is that the checks and balances given to us by our Founding Fathers have become ineffective. The competing interests in our pluralistic society are fueled more by the flaws of human nature than love for our country. Our leaders have deluded us and try to convince us we can sustain ourselves by spending more than we make and that federal planners are more knowledgeable about where we live and what is good for us than local citizens. Businesses are portrayed as the bad guys, even though they are really just us. We should not forget that. We are the workers. We have chosen a system that allows smart and educated leaders who know what they are doing to run the businesses and that encourages financiers to supply the money. We do this because we trust them to perform and provide benefits for us greater than could be obtained from any other system.

This system has made America the greatest engine of production in the world and lifted the standard of living for everyone. Yet, the federal government makes our businesses look bad and, because of the immoral deeds of a few who gain headline notoriety, imposes regulations on all of our businesses, thereby slowing down the great engine of production by making it go uphill. These regulations reinforce an illusion mentality that business is bad and government is good. What is required is balance, which is decided by the people, who can choose to buy or not to buy. No one person, committee, or government can define and achieve the optimum balance necessary to keep our production engine running smoothly without consuming our freedoms. Our freedom to choose is the best regulator, but government is also necessary to prevent fraud and other injuries in appropriate cases.

On this battlefield of ideas, there are many persons competing to be our leaders. Some say they are Democrats or Republicans. Others say they are progressives or liberals or conservatives or neo-conservatives. Yet, nobody but the intellectuals have much of an idea what these terms mean. And whatever each of them stands for likely has some good and some bad. So, waging the contest on a battlefield of nomenclatures is not likely to do much good. I realized this in 1977.

December 1977 was the two-hundredth anniversary of the Revolutionary Army's encampment at Valley Forge. Reports in the paper at the time caused me to pause and reflect on our country and its history. I remembered my dad telling me once that he was summoned for jury duty, and every time someone offered an excuse to get out of it, the judge would say, "Remember the frozen feet at Valley Forge," and the complainants would then sulk back and perform their duty.

I decided not to complain but to do something. I ran for office several times but was not successful. However, the experience did give me an incentive to learn and to use what I had learned, as an architect would do, to fix our country by working on its systems and not competing for authority to exercise the powers they provide or taking the systems for granted.

In 1982 I wrote a business plan for Campaign Constitution, which was not much different than the one I have now. Yet, I could not interest anyone in helping me push this campaign along. I set it aside and went back to being a worker like everyone else. Even so, I continued to collect every idea that crossed my desk on how our Constitution could be improved by amendments and continued to give the subject the benefit of my own thinking.

In the meantime I grew more and more frustrated with our leaders. I remember listening to presidential debates in 1992 between George H. W. Bush and Bill Clinton. In two lengthy debates I heard three offhand references to the word "freedom." In other words, the most important word we have in the governance of our affairs was largely taken for granted, with no comments or questions on the impact any of their ideas might have on our freedom. And if that was true, then the Constitution itself likely was also taken for granted. Twenty years later, we now hear the word "freedom" more often, but it is asserted with little determination.

During the past thirty years the issue in the competition for power has always been how much the government could do for us. It was not about acting on Abe Lincoln's injunction that we should help those who cannot help themselves or defending our country, but how we could have a universal system of social justice that would benefit everyone and, since it was universal, justify taxing everyone. Yet, the actuarial discipline that keeps insurance companies solvent was not a discipline of the federal government as our large national debt now affirms.

So, what was I to do? I could join the ranks of those who take freedom for granted. Or those who hope everything will work out fine. Or those who are resigned to accept whatever may come. Or I could dust off my Campaign Constitution plan and do something about a broken system that few of our leaders address. I decided to do that and allay the fears of those who worry that they or their progeny will someday be like Shukhov, who, while in a Russian labor camp, said that guessing how the authorities would next "twist the law" to extend his sentence was like "pitch-forking water."[2]

What follows is my proposal to fix the system by reforming the Constitution. If you share even a few of the ideas here set forth, I hope you will roll up your sleeves and work on your State legislators to make the changes we so desperately need.

PART 1

CAMPAIGN CONSTITUTION

1

SUMMARY OF
CAMPAIGN CONSTITUTION

Campaign Constitution began with a business plan to change the Constitution through the States and not through Congress. Article V of the Constitution permits two-thirds of the States to convene a Constitutional Convention and to thereafter submit the proposed amendments to the States for ratification either by State constitutional conventions or by their legislatures as determined by Congress.

I began this effort in 1982 and wrote a business plan at that time. I found no interest, which may well also be the case today. I became weary of various emails suggesting changes to the Constitution but with no plan or organized effort to achieve them. I decided to try again. This is a bipartisan effort. Political views are to be shunted aside in favor of the expenditure of common energy to improve our system by correcting imbalances that have developed but were never anticipated by the Founding Fathers, who could not have foreseen the America we live in today.

The alarmists oppose the convention method because of the fear that a Constitutional Convention would open up their sacred document and result in changes to the Bill of Rights, the balance of powers, or other important features of our republican form of government. They have a point. In order to overcome this risk, we have decided that the constitutional resolution to be presented to the Constitutional Convention should be determined in advance and approved in advance by the States and that the Constitutional Convention should be limited to that resolution. This approach would prevent the Constitutional Convention from considering all of the matters that give rise to the fears just described. In other words, it would limit the jurisdiction of the Constitutional Convention by agreement of the States to specified items.

I also knew that none of the changes to the Constitution that I thought appropriate would necessarily be agreed to by others. Many would weigh in on the changes—the way they were worded, their necessity, the purpose of the changes, and so forth. To deal with these objections and to determine whether the changes could take place at all, the business plan proposes developing organizations with bipartisan representation in each of the States and to bring those organizations together in one place to hash out the Constitutional Convention Resolution before taking it back to the States to seek the two-thirds vote requirement necessary to have an official and formal Constitutional Convention. In this fashion, States, informally working together, become the first layer of consensus.

After the informal gathering of State organizations and agreement on a Constitutional Convention Resolution, the resolution would be submitted to each of the State legislatures for approval for the purpose of obtaining a two-thirds vote, which would require Congress to convene the Constitutional Convention. Once the Constitutional Convention has been convened, delegates would be chosen as required by the laws of the various States whose jurisdiction would be limited as specified in the Constitutional Convention Resolution, and there would be an opportunity to decide then what, if anything, would be required to reform our Constitution. The Constitutional Convention Resolution reported by the Constitutional Convention would then be submitted to either the State legislatures for ratification or to conventions of each State for ratification as determined by Congress.

The presentation in this book begins with a summary of the forty-four proposed amendments I have set forth. Following this summary are commentaries on each of the proposed amendments repeating the summary language, repeating the language proposed for the Constitution, and containing comments relevant to the proposed amendment.

Following the commentaries are twelve essays relevant to concerns facing all Americans, for whatever benefit they might have to those interested in joining this most important cause.

At the end of this short book there are appendices containing the Declaration of Independence, the Constitution as it would read if the changes proposed were adopted, a proposed Constitutional Convention Resolution, and my biography.

2

MANAGEMENT

Campaign Constitution is a Colorado nonprofit corporation managed solely by me upon the advice of a fifteen-member Advisory Committee composed of educated scholars who know more about the Constitution and the affairs of men than I do. As of the publication of this book, the only member of the Advisory Committee is my lifelong friend and Masters rowing partner, Michael D. Iseman, M.D., who has distinguished himself in pulmonology and the treatment of tuberculosis and in his concern for the health of our country. In due course, I expect to appoint others to this Advisory Committee, even though I cannot name one of them at this time—nor is it likely that I even know them yet. My thought is that fate will deliver them when the seriousness of the cause becomes established.

Substantially everything in this book will be posted on our website at www.CampaignConstitution.com. Even so, it occurred to me that having this little book available would help educate the public, galvanize support for the cause, and raise funds needed to establish the organizations in the States. It would also provide a more convenient way of referring to proposed changes than opening up a computer from time to time and printing selected commentaries or other information. All proprietary rights to the book shall be assigned to Campaign Constitution. Except for reimbursement of my out-of-pocket expenses duly accounted for, I pledge to receive no remuneration for my time and services on behalf of Campaign Constitution, unless approved by the Advisory Committee.

We will have a policy of complete transparency in terms of receipts and expenditures. We have filed an application with the IRS for a Section 503(c)(4) designation but have not yet received a response. Our governing documents will be posted on the website. Comments of others will be preserved, and links will be provided to other views and information relevant to the task ahead of us.

If our readers share our interest in fixing the system by reforming the Constitution, we hope they will spread the word and make such donations as they are able, establish chapters of interest in their respective communities, and aid in the acceleration of the changes needed to restore the freedoms envisioned by the Founding Fathers.

3

ONE MANAGER ONLY

I will make decisions for Campaign Constitution as long as I am able. I will have the advice and recommendations of an Advisory Committee and arrange for succession if I am unable to act. I acknowledge that more and better ideas can come from group collaboration, but I also recognize that decisions made by an individual avoid unacceptable compromises. Any group suffers from the same infirmities of a government. Alexander Hamilton, in *Federalist No. 15*, said:

> Why has government been instituted at all? Because the passions of men will not conform to the dictates of reason and justice without constraint. Has it been found that bodies of men act with more rectitude or greater disinterestedness than individuals? The contrary of this has been inferred by all accurate observers of the conduct of mankind; and the inference is founded upon obvious reasons. Regard to reputation has a less active influence when the infamy of bad action is to be divided among the number than when it is to fall singly upon one. A spirit of faction, which is apt to

mingle its poison in the deliberations of all bodies of men, will often hurry the persons of whom they are composed into improprieties and excesses for which they would blush in a private capacity.[3]

I have arrived at this decision after great reflection. I am no Pythagoras, Lycurgus, or Solon, but they provide worthy inspiration. I think one can say after review of my life that I am not one who "made the fattest of the milk his own." I am not a specialist. I am not a constitutional law professor. I have written the proposed amendments and related commentaries as a service to our country. I have undoubtedly made mistakes and overlooked important information. But I am confident others will set me straight.

In *The Prince and the Discourses*, Niccolo Machiavelli, a great discerner of human nature, said:

> But we must assume, as a general rule, that it never or rarely happens that a republic or monarchy is well constituted, or its own institutions entirely reformed, unless it is done by only one individual; it is even necessary.[4]

I have also been greatly impressed by the method of decision making employed by Jean de la Valette, Grand Master of the Order of St. John of Jerusalem, who, it is said, managed the knights during the siege of Malta in 1565 by daily meetings where twenty-five knights, representatives of the others, made their views known. A grand council meeting was held on August 23, 1565, where the question was to abandon the Citadel Birgu and retreat to the Citadel St. Angelo to its rear. One of the knights pointed out: "The whole ground near the ruined walls is so honey-combed with the enemy's mines, and our countermines, that one seems to be treading on the crust of a volcano."[5] They thought they would do better to retreat to a more stable citadel than stay in one that had been riddled with artillery shells since May. Ernle Bradford, in *The Great Siege: Malta 1565* (Wordsworth Ed. 1961), reported:

> There was not a single dissentient voice to this plan to withdraw within St. Angelo—except the Grand Master's. Having heard the opinions of his senior Knights, La Valette rose to his feet, "I respect your advice, my brethren—But I shall not take it, and these are my reasons...."[6]

Because of the Grand Master's decision, the five-month siege was shortly thereafter won when the remaining Turks, having lost more than thirty thousand men to approximately 2,500 knights, abandoned the siege. As Bradford concluded,

> At the grand Council meeting that night, the 23rd of August, when the proposal to evacuate Birgu was made, La Valette by his obstinate insistence that there could be no retreat, only confirmed the policy which he had adopted from the very beginning of the siege. His inflexible resolve and his burning belief in the righteousness of his cause, proved the moral backbone which saved Malta.[7]

Today, we are led by those who would have the "fattest of the milk." Leaders want power and want to preserve their standing and reputation as leaders. They invoke principle as an excuse to avoid discourse and harmony. They put their election ahead of their country. Sidney Hook, in *The Hero in History* (1992), said:

> A democracy is imperiled not alone by its heroes, necessary as they may sometimes be for survival. It is imperiled by any group of its citizens who are more attached to the advantages or privileges they enjoy under democracy, or hope it will bring, than they are to the democratic process of bringing them about. For these groups, which set greater store

on peace or prosperity or social status than they do on the methods of democracy to preserve (or modify) them, are the ones which feel justified in calling in the hero to cherish their "goods" even at the cost of democracy.[8]

He also confirmed the importance of vigilance:

A democracy delegates leadership but cannot surrender to it. A democracy—a self-governing republic of citizens with equal rights—must be jealous of the powers it delegates to its leaders; for unless power is limited by other power, it is subject to usurpation and abuse. In a healthy democracy the leader must be more than a mouthpiece of those who select him. He cannot trail after events, or in a world of dizzying change break out the flags and rhetoric of yesteryear to conceal the absence of an adequate program. He must anticipate events, devise policies for the benefit not only of the interests that supported him but for the interests of all. For where there is no vision, a people perishes—particularly in times of danger.

That is why the heroes in a democracy are not likely to be *event-making* men and women unless they subvert the democratic process.[9]

I could go on. My decision has been made. Public leadership is understood by its absence because then institutions, like political parties, the media, religions, and special interests, take over and resolution of controversy requires an unacceptable compromise. By this lesson, one can only conclude that we have no public leadership today. As armies are governed by a single general, so must the reform of a republic. Until I am proved wrong, Campaign Constitution will proceed in earnest to reform our republic and restore the process by which people live together in harmony with reverence for the institutions that have given, and will again give, each of us that proper measure of freedom that supplies to all an equal opportunity to pursue his own happiness.

To learn who I am, please see Appendix E. To understand what I think, please read the Essays.

PART 2

PROPOSED AMENDMENTS

Declaration of Independence by John Trumbull

Scene at the Signing of the Constitution of the United States
by Howard Chandler Christy

SUMMARY OF AMENDMENTS

Amd. No.	Chapter and Amendment Summary

Article I Section 7: Amendment No. 28.

The following Amendment adds additional language to the second paragraph of Section 7 of Article I of the Constitution.

28.0	[Ch. 5]	**Line-Item Veto** The President shall have a line-item veto.

Article I Section 9: Amendment No. 29.

The following Amendments add seven additional paragraphs to Section 9 of Article I of the Constitution.

29.1	[Ch. 6]	**Committee Term Limits** Membership on committees of the House and Senate is limited to four terms in the House and two terms in the Senate.
29.2	[Ch. 7]	**Equity Required** Congress shall equitably treat government employees and retired congressmen and senators if they lose their health and other pension benefits by amendment to the Constitution.
29.3	[Ch. 8]	**Congressional Compensation** Congressional compensation is to be determined by a committee separate from Congress.

Amd. No.		Chapter and Amendment Summary
29.4	[Ch. 9]	**Public Voting** Earmarks shall be abolished by requiring that Congress shall not pass any law without a vote, and all votes are to be public, recorded, and published.
29.5	[Ch. 10]	**No Pigeonholing** One-third of the members of each House shall have the right to have a vote by their House on any bill, whether in committee or not.
29.6	[Ch. 11]	**Timely Budgets** Annual budgets will be approved in a timely manner and, if not, all of the then-elected members of Congress shall not be qualified to hold elective office after the expiration of their terms.
29.7	[Ch. 12]	**Emergency Bills** No non-emergency bill or amendment shall be tacked onto an emergency bill.

Article I Section 11: Amendment No. 30.

Article I has ten sections. The following Amendments add a new Section 11 containing twelve paragraphs to Article I of the Constitution.

30.1	[Ch. 13]	**Super Majority** A 60 percent vote in both Houses is necessary to raise or spend money.
30.2	[Ch. 14]	**No Retroactivity** Congress shall pass no retroactive bills, civil or criminal, without a two-thirds vote and without an express statement that retroactivity is in the public interest, does not take or impair vested rights, and does not create new obligations or impose new duties prior to the effective date of the bill, except Congress shall never impose any tax retroactively.
30.3	[Ch. 15]	**Tax Changes Prospective** There shall be no increase in the income tax before January 1 of the year following adoption of the increase without a two-thirds vote of both Houses, and there shall be no income tax for a stated term.
30.4	[Ch. 16]	**Limit Mandates** No future mandate shall be imposed upon the States or subdivisions thereof without their consent.

Amd. No.		Chapter and Amendment Summary
30.5	[Ch. 17]	**Campaign Freedom** There shall be no restrictions on the amount of political contributions or expenditures made in connection with federal elections or issues as long as they are promptly disclosed.
30.6	[Ch. 18]	**Preamble for All Laws** Every law shall contain a declaration of purpose, a statement of the constitutional power relied on, and other statements helpful to citizens.
30.7	[Ch. 19]	**No State Bailouts** Congress shall pass no law to purchase (i.e., bail out States) State debts unless the purchase is ratable based on population for all States or unless approved by a two-thirds vote of both Houses.
30.8	[Ch. 20]	**No Exemptions for Congress** Congress shall not exempt itself from any law.
30.9	[Ch. 21]	**Spending Limit** Congress shall not appropriate monies greater than 20 percent of GDP without a two-thirds vote of both Houses.
30.10	[Ch. 22]	**No Special Benefits** Congress shall have no retirement, health, or other pension benefit law for itself or federal employees, except the military, unless the law applies to everyone.
30.11	[Ch. 23]	**No Presidential Spending Authority** Congress shall not delegate spending authority to the President.

Article II Section 2: Amendment No. 31.

This amendment is added to the end of the second paragraph of Section 2 of Article II of the Constitution.

31.0	[Ch. 24]	**Timely Appointments** The President and Senate shall act in a timely manner on the President's appointment of judges, ambassadors, and other public ministers or they shall not be paid.

Amd. No.	Chapter and Amendment Summary	

Article II Section 5: Amendment No. 32.

Article II has four sections. The following amendments add five paragraphs to a new Section 5 to Article II of the Constitution.

32.1	[Ch. 25]	**Prioritize Agencies** The President shall prioritize all federal agencies with a number to resolve conflicts between agencies and preserve the rule of law.
32.2	[Ch. 26]	**Limit Agency Authority** Congress's delegation of legislative authority to federal agencies shall be strictly construed.
32.3	[Ch. 27]	**No Retroactive Regulations** Proposed agency regulations shall have no effect until finally approved.
32.4	[Ch. 28]	**No Multiple Applications** Applications for federal permits shall be made to one agency only and ruled upon promptly.
32.5	[Ch. 29]	**President Answers Questions** Upon request of the House of Representatives, the President shall appear before it while in session to answer questions but not more often than weekly and for not more than forty minutes for each appearance.

Article V: Amendment No. 33.

Article V has one paragraph. The following amendments add two additional paragraphs to Article V of the Constitution.

33.1	[Ch. 30]	**Constitutional Amendments by States** A majority of State legislatures shall have the right to submit amendments to the Constitution to the States for ratification by three-fourths of the States.
33.2	[Ch. 31]	**Save Bill of Rights** Amendments to the Bill of Rights or the Thirteenth, Fourteenth, and Fifteenth Amendments shall not be authorized without unanimous approval of all the States.

Amd. No.	Chapter and Amendment Summary

Article VI: Amendment No. 34.

Article VI has three paragraphs. The following amendments add five additional paragraphs to Article VI of the Constitution.

34.1	[Ch. 32]	**Voting Tax** As a condition to the right to vote in a federal election, every citizen shall annually pay an equal tax sufficient to raise revenues necessary to operate Congress, provided the tax shall begin at $10 and, when changed, shall never be more than the cost of one-fourth of one troy ounce of silver.
34.2	[Ch. 33]	**Limited Number of Regulations** Federal regulations cannot exceed four times the size of federal statutes.
34.3	[Ch. 34]	**Limited Life of Regulations** Federal regulations shall automatically be void ten years after their adoption unless earlier approved by Congress for a stated term.
34.4	[Ch. 35]	**Limit Number of Congressional Staff** Congressional staff shall be limited to twenty-five thousand persons unless increased by a majority vote of the State legislatures upon the request of Congress.
34.5	[Ch. 36]	**UFO Full Disclosure** No government person shall suppress information regarding UFOs.

Tenth Amendment: Amendment No. 35. The Tenth

Amendment contains one paragraph. The following amendments amend this paragraph and add four more sections to Amendment X of the Constitution.

35.1	[Ch. 37]	**Reinvigorate the Tenth Amendment** The States or the people shall have all powers not delegated to Congress by the Constitution whether existing before or arising because of the Constitution.
35.2	[Ch. 38]	**Term Limits** State legislatures shall have the power to limit the terms of members of Congress in their States.
35.3	[Ch. 39]	**State Repeal of Federal Laws** Two-thirds of the state legislatures have the power to repeal a federal law.

Amd. No.		Chapter and Amendment Summary
35.4	[Ch. 40]	**Board of Governors** There shall exist a Board of Governors (State governors) to assist States in the exercise of their powers under the Constitution.
35.5	[Ch. 41]	**Legislatures Defined** Approval by each State legislature means majority approval by all members of each House in the State's legislative branch.

Amendment No. 36.

The following amendments add seven sections to the Constitution.

36.1	[Ch. 42]	**Jury Decides Unreasonableness of Government Action** Whether any law is unconstitutional as applied (i.e., arbitrary and unreasonable under the circumstances) is a question of fact for a jury.
36.2	[Ch. 43]	**More Citizen Standing** Every citizen shall have standing in court to seek the meaning of the Constitution or to challenge the constitutionality or validity of any federal law or regulation or to seek a declaration of the meaning thereof.
36.3	[Ch. 44]	***Mens Rea* Required** No person shall be guilty of a federal crime unless the person's *mens rea* has been proved beyond a reasonable doubt.
36.4	[Ch. 45]	**No Severance Clause** If any part of a bill that becomes law is determined to be unconstitutional, the whole law shall be unconstitutional.
36.5	[Ch. 46]	**State Legislatures Elect U.S. Senators** The Seventeenth Amendment to the Constitution requiring the direct election of Senators shall be repealed.
36.6	[Ch. 47]	**Limit Congressional Power** The "general Welfare" clause as used in the preamble of the Constitution does not grant Congress any power and as used in Article I § 8 grants power exercisable only by at least a two-thirds vote of both Houses.

Amd. No.		Chapter and Amendment Summary
36.7	[Ch. 48]	**Limit Executive Privilege** Doubts as to whether the President can lawfully assert executive privilege on any matter to avoid releasing information to Congress shall be resolved against the President.

James Madison, March 16,1751-June 28,1836

5

AMENDMENT NO. 28: LINE-ITEM VETO

SUMMARY

28.0   The President shall have a line-item veto.

COMMENTS

Congress routinely includes in spending bills appropriations that the President would prefer not to spend. However, the general consensus is that he must accept all of a bill as law or none of it. The result is that he must compare the overall benefits of a bill to its disadvantages before he signs. If the President signs the bill, he is duty bound to spend the funds he would prefer not to spend. The overall consequence is that the President is denied the opportunity to manage the financial affairs of the nation in the best way he can. If the President decides to veto the bill, Congress by a two-thirds vote can always override the President and force the spending.

In *Denton v. City of New York*, 524 U.S. 417 (1998), the Supreme Court said the Line-Item Veto Act passed by Congress was not constitutional since it violated the procedures required by the Constitution to pass laws.

Most people confronted with this issue favor a line-item veto as a check on Congress prompted by lack of confidence that Congress will act wisely, and, accordingly, we have submitted it for consideration by the States. This proposed amendment in effect requires a two-thirds vote of Congress if it wants to preserve as law those items in an appropriation bill objected to by the President.

CONSTITUTIONAL LANGUAGE

Every bill not an appropriation bill which shall have passed the House of Representatives and the Senate shall, before it becomes a law, be presented to the President of the United States. If he approves he shall sign it, but if not, he shall return it with his objections to the House in which it shall have originated, which shall enter the objections at large on its journal and proceed to reconsider it. If after such reconsideration two-thirds of that House shall agree to pass the bill, it shall be sent, together with the objections, to the other House, by which it shall likewise be reconsidered, and if approved by two-thirds of that House, it shall become a law. Every appropriation bill which shall have passed the House of Representatives and the Senate shall, before it becomes law, be presented to the President of the United States; if he approves, he shall sign it, but if he approves it in part, he shall sign it as to the sections approved and shall return the bill with the parts not approved with his objections to that House in which it shall have originated, which shall thereupon proceed in the manner provided for above with respect to bills which are not appropriation bills. If the parts objected to are not approved as there provided, such parts shall not be law, but the parts approved shall be law.

6

Amendment No. 29.1: Committee Term Limits

SUMMARY

29.1 Membership on committees of the House and Senate is limited to four terms in the House and two terms in the Senate.

COMMENT

Many people have complained about the powers of congressional committees (and their entrenched staff), particularly those whose chairmen have dominated their proceedings for many years. While other changes to the Constitution we have recommended may moot this complaint, we are offering this proposal to ensure that committee power is diminished.

CONSTITUTIONAL LANGUAGE

No member of any committee of Congress shall serve on such committee longer than four terms in the House and two terms in the Senate as those terms are defined in Sections 1 and 2 of Article I of the Constitution.

Alexander Hamilton, June 11,1755-July 12, 1804

AMENDMENT NO. 29.2: EQUITY REQUIRED

SUMMARY

29.2 Congress shall equitably treat government employees and retired congressmen and senators if they lose their health and other pension benefits by amendment to the Constitution.

COMMENT

As a matter of fairness, we have provided in this proposed amendment a method for dealing equitably with members of Congress and federal employees who have relied on existing law for their retirement. This method gives Congress two years from the adoption of proposed amendment 30.10 (Chapter 22) to calculate the present value of the future benefits of these persons and to thereafter pay such persons in cash or over time as Congress shall determine. Some may say the 10 percent discount rate applied to the actuarial determination is too high. However, it is close to long-term yields in the stock market. These congressional and federal beneficiaries of special programs should not be heard to complain based upon short-term economic conditions for which they are largely responsible.

CONSTITUTIONAL LANGUAGE

Any existing Law in conflict with the Twenty-Ninth Amendment shall be void except any law in conflict with Clause 10 of the Twenty-Ninth Amendment shall not be void until two years after its adoption, during which time Congress shall extinguish all prohibited benefits and pay or promise to pay the present value thereof determined actuarially using a discount rate of 10 percent per annum, as of the date of such adoption, to those whose benefits are terminated thereby, with any deferred payment made without interest on such terms and conditions and over such time as Congress shall establish.

8

AMENDMENT NO. 29.3: CONGRESSIONAL COMPENSATION

SUMMARY

29.3   Congressional compensation is to be determined by a committee separate from Congress.

COMMENT

Congressional compensation is a favorite political issue. We even have Amendment 27 to the Constitution, which prohibits members of Congress from varying their pay until a congressional election has intervened. No one wants to be seen as increasing his pay while a member of Congress, thereby also being seen as using his political power to pad his pocketbook. The political fear that this reluctance imposes has generated consequences significantly more adverse than a congressman increasing his pay. It has deterred from the ranks of Congress those who cannot afford to serve because of low salaries. Second, it has generated an incentive in congressmen to find other ways, sometimes devious and criminal, to increase their remuneration. For example, we find as late as 2011 that Congress does not have restrictions on the ability of its members to take advantage of information unique to them in buying and selling stocks. Third, we hear stories about persons going into Congress as ordinary people but coming out as millionaires. Lastly, we generate a climate where wealthy patricians become the unique class of persons able to run and serve in Congress. There are likely many more arguments against the current system by which Congress compensates itself.

We believe the system can be much improved by establishing a separate committee to compensate Congress and to make it invulnerable to any influence by Congress. In all likelihood, the committee would increase congressional pay to provide incentives for increasing the quality and intelligence of better leaders in Washington, D.C.

It is often said that former Minnesota Senator Hubert Humphrey was the model of a public servant because he came out of Congress after many years of service with no more than he had when he went in. This should be the standard of a person whose fidelity to the country is his top priority.

CONSTITUTIONAL LANGUAGE

Direct and indirect compensation for members of Congress shall be equal. Compensation for members of Congress and their staff shall be established every four years beginning on the first day of the second calendar year following the effective date of the adoption of this amendment by a majority vote of a committee of six, two appointed by Congress, two by the President, and two by a majority vote of the governors of the several States, one each for a term of two years and one each for a term of four years with appointments made in like manner every two years for a term of four years. Committee deadlocks lasting more than thirty days shall be resolved by the President upon application of any committee member. Such committee shall have the power to appropriate from the federal treasury such funds as shall be required to perform its duties, including the compensation and expenses of the members thereof, which shall be of public record and never exceed for a committee member the amount established for a member of Congress proportionally reduced to his time of actual service. Appropriations to cover all other costs of operating Congress are reserved to Congress.

Amendment No. 29.4: Public Voting

SUMMARY

29.4   Earmarks shall be abolished by requiring that
       Congress shall not pass any law without a vote,
       and all votes are to be public, recorded, and
       published.

COMMENT

Earmarks are a form of special legislation—that is, the legislation benefits a few people but not the people generally. They are frequently approved in conference committee to avoid debate. In effect, Congress directs that a certain amount of an agency's budget be spent on specific projects, thereby removing discretion over the funds from others. Earmarks are synonymous with what we call "pork barrel projects."

State constitutions and by implication the U.S. Constitution prohibit special legislation. Special legislation is, in effect, conferring legislative favors on some and not on others. The courts have consistently validated what appears to be special legislation if the beneficiaries fall within a classification deemed reasonable. Thus, for example, in Colorado commercial property is taxed at a higher rate than residential property because the classification of the two is deemed reasonable.

Earmarks are a classic form of special legislation by which Congress confers favors on its members in exchange for votes. We have all heard about the "bridge to nowhere" in Alaska. Most members of Congress are publicly against earmarks, but they continue to approve them unabashedly. Through legislative sleight of hand, earmarks are permitted because voting on them is usually obscured to shield our representatives from accountability.

Would a constitutional amendment opposing special legislation solve the problem? Although such a rule might solve the problem, it would also lead to ingenious classification strategies and result in considerable litigation. For that reason, we have elected to remedy this problem not with a prohibition on special legislation, but with a requirement that there be a publicly recorded vote on every appropriation bill. In this fashion, members of Congress who oppose earmarks can offer amendments to delete them and force a vote on the amendment, which, in due course, will allow citizens the opportunity to vote against persons who say they oppose earmarks yet vote for them. Also, if the President has a line-item veto, he is in a position to be rid of them and acts at his political peril by approving them.

Voting discipline is another way of eliminating earmarks. Congress currently passes laws by different means, including a show of hands, voice votes, and roll-call votes. The roll-call vote is the only method by which a member of Congress has his vote for or against a measure officially recorded and published. In the old days, other means of voting were appropriate because of the time required to vote. Today, however, with the electronic and technological improvements that have occurred, voting on any issue is as simple as pushing a button. By requiring recorded votes on all measures, members of Congress lose the ability to hide behind the shield of an unaccountable vote or avoid taking the position on a matter deemed important enough to be voted upon by Congress. People were not elected to Congress to vote "present" but to be leaders for their country and their State and to take positions. Those positions should be known and recorded so that we have a healthy government.

CONSTITUTIONAL LANGUAGE

All bills and each and every provision thereof or amendment thereto shall be passed by Congress as provided in the Constitution by votes, and all votes shall be public, be recorded, and be published by voter.

10

Amendment No. 29.5: No Pigeonholing

SUMMARY

29.5   One-third of the members of each House shall
have the right to have a vote by their House on any
bill, whether in committee or not.

COMMENT

It is common knowledge that the rules of both the House and the
Senate give authority to certain individuals to prevent a bill from
being presented for a vote by the members of either the House or
the Senate. In many cases, there are likely sound political reasons for
such a rule, but, in all cases, this rule means that a particular bill is
held in committee and will not be released until somebody else supplies an undesirable *quid pro quo*.

In order to put the country's interests first, it seems appropriate
that if one-third of the members of either House determine that a
bill should be voted on by the whole House, regardless of whether
the bill has been reported by the committee, then they can act by this

rule to force the bill from the committee and present it for a vote by their House.

CONSTITUTIONAL LANGUAGE

One-third of the members of each House shall have the right to have a vote by their House on any bill whether in committee or not.

11

AMENDMENT NO. 29.6: TIMELY BUDGETS

SUMMARY

29.6   Annual budgets will be approved in a timely manner and, if not, all of the then-elected members of Congress shall not be qualified to hold elective office after the expiration of their terms.

COMMENT

Nothing invites more disrespect for Congress than its inability to manage the country's financial affairs. This Amendment will penalize federally elected representatives and senators severely by forbidding all of them from running for public office in the future in the event they fail to adopt budgets meaningful to our citizens in a timely manner.

The proposed amendment will also require that budgets be compared to the prior year's budget on both a cash and accrual basis, which will give more information to citizens and allow them to know whether liabilities are building up on an accrual basis in the management of the federal government.

CONSTITUTIONAL LANGUAGE

Both Houses shall agree on a budget for the succeeding year no later than October 1 of the prior year, failing which none of the members thereof shall be qualified to hold elective office in Congress after the expiration of his or her then existing term of office. All future budgets shall be compared to the current year's budget on both a cash and accrual basis, and such comparison shall be part of the budget.

12

AMENDMENT NO. 29.7: EMERGENCY BILLS

SUMMARY

29.7   No non emergency bill or amendment shall be tacked onto an emergency bill.

COMMENT

It is a common practice when an emergency bill is required to help certain of our beleaguered citizens with the consequences of weather and other perils for representatives and senators to tack onto that bill their favorite program, deal, or pork barrel project. This amendment will prevent that practice and limit emergency bills to matters related to the emergency.

CONSTITUTIONAL LANGUAGE

No emergency appropriation bill whose purpose is to prevent or mitigate or respond to a loss of life or property or a threat to national security shall be valid if it contains any non-emergency spending authorization.

13

AMENDMENT NO. 30.1: SUPER MAJORITY

SUMMARY

30.1   A 60 percent vote in both Houses is necessary to raise or spend money.

COMMENT

One of the biggest weaknesses of a democracy is the tyranny of the majority. Our Constitution attempted to guard against the tyranny of the majority by creating a republican form of government. This was based on the assumption that elected representatives would work together to pursue goals that are in the best interests of the country. Yet, the record shows that most elected leaders are more interested in continuing in power or advancing their personal ambitions than in pursuing the interests of the country. Any survey of what has occurred in America illustrates that this is exactly what has happened.

Politicians putting their own interests ahead of those of the country has resulted in a highly polarized system of government pursuant to which the victor at the polls, even though achieving victory by only a few percentage points, claims a mandate of support for the particular platform that formed the basis for his reelection. The polarization that has occurred from this phenomenon has made it impossible for the political parties to work together and has generated an opportunity for the minority to make claims that it would never make if it were in power and accountable for the consequences of its positions.

We have to remember that politicians advocate policies that they represent to be in the public interest but that at the same time assure their reelection. These policies, as we have discerned in these commentaries, generate a plethora of unintended consequences. Policy making is a hazardous business and should be cautiously exercised.

The illusion that the victor at the polls represents the country is illustrated by voting data over the past fifty years as recorded by Congress. We have assembled this data, which illustrate that not a single elected President, representative, or senator in the last fifty years has received a majority of the votes of the citizens of the United States who are qualified to vote.

While it is lamentable that many Americans simply do not register to vote or, if registered, do not vote, it cannot be accepted as true that those who do vote represent the majority or that the successful candidate has a mandate from the majority. Because of this, every elected representative becomes a fiduciary not only for those who have chosen not to vote but also for the young who are not yet of voting age, who represent an estimated 24 percent of the citizen population.

In order to honor the fiduciary obligation associated with the young and those who do not vote, all elected representatives have a duty to consider not only their own platforms but the platforms that all the people would find acceptable and in their short-term and long-term best interests. In order to do this, we believe a 60 percent vote on taxing and appropriation bills is an essential reminder that a majority of elected representatives do not have an unaccountable power and represent not just their constituency but all Americans. In like manner, it requires that minorities not be intransient in their opposition to the majority in power but work together. In fact, a 60 percent vote requirement will likely foster minority parties that, upon forming coalitions with other parties, will give minorities more influence and increase overall accountability.

Proactive harmony is a recipe for a more holistic view of American interests and honors the gift from Hermes as related by Protagoras in Plato's writings and quoted in the Preface.

CONSTITUTIONAL LANGUAGE

Congress shall have no power to pass any bill for raising revenue or for appropriating money unless it is approved by three-fifths of both Houses.

14

AMENDMENT NO. 30.2: NO RETROACTIVITY

SUMMARY

30.2 Congress shall pass no retroactive bills, civil or criminal, without a two-thirds vote and without an express statement that retroactivity is in the public interest, does not take or impair vested rights, and does not create new obligations or impose new duties prior to the effective date of the bill, except Congress shall never impose any tax retroactively.

COMMENT

The notion that a law could somehow apply retroactively has been universally condemned and is currently covered by Article I, § 10 of the Constitution ("No Bill of Attainder or ex post facto law shall be passed"). States are prohibited from passing an "ex post facto law, or law impairing the obligation of Contracts...." James Madison argued that retroactive legislation offered special opportunities for the powerful to obtain special and improper benefits. However, the Supreme Court has interpreted these constitutional provisions to apply only to penal litigation.

In *Landgraf v. USI Film Products*, 511 U.S. 244 (1994), the Supreme Court cited an earlier case that "Congressional enactments and administrative rules will not be considered to have retroactive effect unless their language requires this result." The court said the Constitution only prohibited penal retroactivity and therefore permitted other types of retroactivity when congressional intent was clear.

Although it may be appropriate in some cases to have retroactive laws (emergencies or to correct clear mistakes), they should certainly not be passed unless a super majority of Congress expressly recognizes why they are important. For this reason a two-thirds vote has been specified as required to achieve the level of unanimity required to meet the expectations of governmental fair dealing with the public.

With respect to taxation, Congress has taken the position that once a bill has been filed and the content of the law becomes known, it is fair to pass the law at a later date but make it effective at an earlier date. Most people disapprove of this practice.

Every day people make decisions and take actions according to the law as it then exists. The idea that Congress can somehow change the mix of facts with a retroactive law and thereby impose a greater burden on the decision maker than existed at the time of the decision is morally wrong. Some persons will take the risk. Other persons will do nothing until the matter is settled in Congress. This delay interdicts economic growth in numerous and unforeseeable ways not predictable by anyone, including Congress.

If Congress wants to raise taxes, it should get about it quickly and efficiently. It should not pull the rug out from underneath the people who make decisions on existing law before a new law is passed.

CONSTITUTIONAL LANGUAGE

Congress shall have no power to pass any retroactive bill unless approved by a two-thirds vote of both Houses except Congress shall never impose taxes retroactively.

Thomas Jefferson, April 13, 1743-July 4,1826

15

AMENDMENT NO. 30.3: TAX CHANGES PROSPECTIVE

SUMMARY

30.3   There shall be no increase in the income tax before January 1 of the year following adoption of the increase without a two-thirds vote of both Houses, and there shall be no income tax for a stated term.

COMMENT

Our comments (Amendment 30.2 Commentary, Chapter 14) with respect to retroactive tax bills are somewhat applicable to this proposed amendment. Since most people do their planning on a yearly basis, it is fair that they should be able to know in advance what the laws will be for a particular year, most especially tax laws that have such a significant influence on economic planning. It stands to reason that if Congress wants to change the income tax laws in a particular year, it should not make those laws effective until the first of the following year. Yet, Congress, in enacting general revenue statutes, has almost without exception given such laws an effective date prior to the date of enactment. The Supreme Court has authorized this practice, holding that it does not violate due process if reasonable (*U.S. v. Darusmont,* 449 U.S. 292 (1981)). Our lives and decisions should not be made to depend on whether judges think retroactive tax laws are reasonable. The Supreme Court has also held that treasury regulations may be retroactively applied unless doing so constitutes an abuse of discretion (*Automobile Club of Michigan v. Commissioner,* 353 U.S. 180, 184 (1957)).

In addition, Congress should not be allowed to make income tax laws for a stated term. The reason is that business planners have no idea what will occur at the expiration of the term. This uncertainty means that they must either assume the risk of a favorable change at the end of the term or go to the sidelines and wait for an answer. It is risk enough that people make their economic decisions knowing that Congress can pass a law at any time that may prove their decisions to have been incorrect. To compound that risk with other risks, such as taxes for a stated term, will have nothing but a deleterious effect upon our economy and ameliorative effect on the ability of elected representatives to shirk their responsibility for political reasons.

CONSTITUTIONAL LANGUAGE

Congress shall have no power to pass any bill using its power under the Sixteenth Amendment that is effective before the first day of the calendar year following its enactment without a two-thirds vote of both Houses, and no such bill shall ever be made subject to a stated term.

16

AMENDMENT NO. 30.4: LIMIT MANDATES

SUMMARY

30.4   No future mandate shall be imposed upon the States or subdivisions thereof without their consent.

COMMENT

When a citizen queries elected leaders from States down to county commissioners, he will find one of their greatest objections is the mandates imposed upon them by the federal government. These mandates require local governments to spend money to achieve policy goals established by Congress without their consent. Not only is this unfair as a practical matter, but it also denies the people the diversity of decision making intended by federalism, prevents the States from planning themselves, and denies them the ability to predict the financial consequences of their own decisions.

Congress itself has recognized this problem by adopting the Unfunded Mandates Reform Act of 1995, designed to end the imposition, in the absence of full consideration by Congress, of federal mandates on State governments without adequate federal funding in a manner that displaces other State governmental priorities. This law has been helpful (see *Printz v. United States,* 521 U.S. 898 (1997)), although we are reminded that Congress could repeal it at any time. This insult to the power and responsibility of State and local governments needs to be brought to an end. Because there currently exist mandates of the sort to be prohibited, we have provided that the amendment be limited to future mandates. Existing mandates can be continued or repealed as determined by Congress.

CONSTITUTIONAL LANGUAGE

Congress shall have no power, after the adoption of this amendment, to impose an enforceable duty upon State, local, or tribal governments or entities by which they do business without their written consent or to discriminate against them in the provision of federal assistance, financial or otherwise, because they refuse to consent.

17

AMENDMENT NO. 30.5: CAMPAIGN FREEDOM

SUMMARY

30.5   There shall be no restrictions on the amount of political contributions or expenditures made in connection with federal elections or issues as long as they are promptly disclosed.

COMMENT

Few issues provoke as much controversy as the money spent in politics. The result is that Congress has enacted laws limiting the amount of contributions using the Federal Election Commission as the policeman. The Federal Election Act of 1971 (amended in 1974) was ruled on by the Supreme Court in *Buckley v. Valeo*, 424 U.S. 1 (1976). The Supreme Court said that a candidate could spend as much of his own money as he wanted but that other people could not contribute more to his campaign than a specified amount. Corporations and labor unions were prohibited from making contributions. The Supreme Court justified its ruling on candidates based upon their First Amendment rights and justified the second part of its decision on a perception, not a fact, that too much money would lead to corruption and that it was a valid governmental interest to prevent corruption or the appearance of corruption. The court later extended this governmental interest to preventing distortion caused by wealth.

In 2002 Congress passed amendments to the law barring corporations and unions from making independent electioneering expenditures. In 2010 the Supreme Court in *Citizens United v. Federal Election Commission*, 130 S. Ct. 876 (2010), ruled that corporations were allowed to make independent political expenditures without limitation. In doing so, the court, relying on *Federalist No. 10* (Madison) ("destroying the liberty [of some factions is] worse than the disease"),[11] concluded that independent corporate expenditure was a free speech right and did not give rise to corruption or its appearance and that the distortion argument was likewise unfounded.

In *Western Tradition Partnership, Inc. v. Attorney General*, 271 P.3d 1 (Mont. 2011), the Montana supreme court reversed a lower court which found that Montana's statutory restriction on corporate donations was unconstitutional. The relevant issues were succinctly raised by the court's comments:

> *Citizens United* was a case decided upon its facts, and involved "unique and complex" rules that affected 71 distinct entities and included separate rule for 33 different types of speech in Federal elections. Since 1975, the Federal Election Commission adopted 568 pages of regulations, 1,278 pages of explanatory materials, and 1,771 advisory opinions to implement and enforce the Federal law. The FEC adopted a two-part, 11-factor test in response to the holding in a single Supreme Court decision. If parties want to avoid litigation and possible penalties they must either refrain from political speech or seek an advisory opinion. All of this, the Supreme Court found, allows the FEC to "select what political speech is safe for public consumption by applying ambiguous tests."

Citizens United, 130 S.Ct. at 895-96. The Court determined that the law was "an outright ban, backed by criminal sanctions." *Citizens United*, 130 S.Ct. at 897.

* * *

While *Citizens United* was decided under its facts or lack of facts, it applied the long-standing rule that restrictions upon speech are not per se unlawful, but rather may be upheld if the government demonstrates a sufficiently strong interest. *Citizens United*, 130 S.Ct. at 898.

After analyzing the facts in Montana, the court found that the Montana government had demonstrated a "sufficiently strong interest" to justify its statute. It is somewhat disheartening to think that a corporation, to protect its First Amendment rights, must litigate amidst a morass of rules to determine its rights when, in the last analysis, some one or few individuals will have the right to decide whether a "sufficiently strong interest" has been established by the government.

Money in politics is not a recent problem. Fifth-century Greeks had major concerns that the monied interests (oligarchies) would take over if not checked. They protected themselves by limiting the power of office holders, not restricting the use of their money. Paul Woodruff in *First Democracy* (2005) said, "Because the Athenians wanted to curb the power of wealth, they severely restricted the powers of those who held elected office. So the representative bodies in Athens were filled not by elections, but by a lottery that drew from a large panel of citizens…such a body would be too large to bribe…."[12] The Roman republic weakened in its latter days because of the influence of monied interests and a corresponding diminishment of the rule of law.

Apart from the law, the facts are clear. It is likely a feature of human nature that no matter what the law is money will show up to influence elections. This is especially true as long as people have a monetary interest in the decisions of Congress. The Supreme Court acknowledged this to be the case in *Citizens United*. Because of this the existing restriction on the amount citizens can contribute to a candidate is likely unconstitutional. Candidates should not be shackled in their effort to rebut claims made by independent organizations under *Citizens United*.

We believe that as long as contributions and expenditures are published promptly voters can deal with this information in a responsible way and that the existing layers of law and regulation serve only to obfuscate who is really behind a particular candidate. Moreover, the complexity of election rules chills the number of candidates willing to run. It is a grim observation that no person should run for federal office without a good lawyer and a good accountant. We cannot be proud that the hurdles facing candidates for federal office deny us many potentially good leaders.

Another important fact is that before the Federal Election Act people (not corporations by reason of the 1907 Tillman Act) were free to make such contributions to federal political candidates as they thought appropriate. Even then, when there were no disclosure requirements, there were no celebrated cases of fraud at the federal level to our knowledge. Today, *potential* fraud and corruption seem to be the primary argument for why government regulation should apply.

The fact is no one knows whether a policy of unlimited contributions would be good or bad. Are we to assume that the average voter is incapable of resisting the persuasive content of political advertisements? You may not like big money in politics but are you willing to admit that you, a sovereign voter, are powerless to overcome its consequences? What is wrong with allowing American people to make up their own minds? If you disagree, you have to believe the average voter cannot be trusted to make up his own mind. This requires that you select some other person to make it up for him. This is the end of freedom and the best case for doing away with democracy all together. This also explains James Madison's comment above.

CONSTITUTIONAL LANGUAGE

Congress shall have no power to pass any bill limiting the amount of contributions by any United States domiciliary corporation or organization or citizen to any corporation, organization, or person for political purposes involving federal policy or federal candidates nor limiting the expenditures of any of the foregoing as long as both the contributions and expenditures are fully and promptly disclosed to the public by the most public and technological means available for such purpose.

18

AMENDMENT NO. 30.6: PREAMBLE FOR ALL LAWS

SUMMARY

30.6   Every law shall contain a declaration of purpose, a statement of the constitutional power relied on, and other statements helpful to citizens.

COMMENT

Every bill passed by Congress that becomes law implicitly contains a representation by Congress that it has the constitutional power to make the law, that the law is in the best interests of the United States, that the United States can afford the law, that the law has a purpose, and that the range of unintended consequences is dominated by the contemplated benefits.

Congress should be made to include in every bill a declaration stating expressly what is obviously implied. Each of these declarations would allow competing political candidates to contrast their positions on specific legislation with the position of the incumbent. Further, an elected person who consistently supports measures that turn out to have been ill advised becomes a questionable leader de-spite the genuineness of his decisions.

CONSTITUTIONAL LANGUAGE

Congress shall have no power to pass any bill unless it sets forth at the beginning thereof a declaration of the purpose thereof and the constitutional power under which it is brought, a statement that the bill is needed for the public interest, a statement that the government can afford the bill, a statement that the government can administer the bill in a way people can respect, a statement of its impact on the freedoms of citizens, and a statement of its possible unintended consequences.

19

Amendment No. 30.7: No State Bailouts

SUMMARY

30.7 Congress shall pass no law to purchase (i.e., bail out States) State debts unless the purchase is ratable based on population for all States or unless approved by a two-thirds vote of both Houses.

COMMENT

Any effort by Congress to bail out any person, business, or State is a form of special legislation. In 1980 Congress bailed out Chrysler and did not lose any money in the process. The justification was a classification founded on the theory of "too big to fail." In 2009 Congress bailed out Wall Street under the same theory, with a large consensus being that it was a waste of money and did more harm than good. At the same time, Congress bailed out General Motors on the "too big to fail" theory, but the jury is still out on whether taxpayers will recover all of the $50 billion in equity, $6.7 billion loan, and $18 billion in tax breaks furnished to that company to allow it to continue under reputedly uneconomical contracts.

There has been discussion about bailing out certain States, like California, that have mismanaged their economy to the point that they may go bankrupt. One can imagine the classification dreamed up to support a congressional "too big to fail" bailout of California, namely GDP produced by the State, importance of the State to the national interest, and similar arguments. Yet, most people believe this is wrong. The purpose of this amendment is to ensure that States are not bailed out unless two-thirds of both Houses agree. States need to conduct themselves responsibly or face the consequences.

CONSTITUTIONAL LANGUAGE

Congress shall have no power to provide financial assistance to, or purchase any debt securities of, any State or entity by which it does business or subdivisions or municipalities thereof unless the financial assistance or purchase is provided to all States and prorated by population determined by the most recent census or unless approved by a two-thirds vote of both Houses.

AMENDMENT NO. 30.8:
NO EXEMPTIONS FOR CONGRESS

SUMMARY

30.8   Congress shall not exempt itself from any law.

COMMENT

It is common knowledge that Congress exempts itself from numerous laws that it imposes on Americans generally. Some of these laws are OSHA, the Freedom of Information Act, the National Labor Relations Act, and the Civil Rights Act. James Madison said that Congress "can make no law which will not have its full operation on themselves and their friends, as well as on the great mass of society."[13]

Most people believe Congress should live by the same laws that it imposes upon others. This amendment assures that result.

CONSTITUTIONAL LANGUAGE

Congress shall have no power to exempt itself from any law or be separately classified so as to be treated differently from the people generally.

21

AMENDMENT NO. 30.9: SPENDING LIMIT

SUMMARY

30.9 Congress shall not appropriate monies greater than 20 percent of GDP without a two-thirds vote of both Houses.

COMMENT

This amendment is as close as we have come to a balance-the-budget amendment. The trouble with a requirement that the budget be balanced is that it denies flexibility to Congress to deal with unforeseeable circumstances that require occasional borrowing. In fact, it was the availability of credit that permitted Henry Ford to grow Ford Motor Company into the business that it is today. It would be unfair to the American people to deny Congress the ability to use credit vehicles in appropriate cases.

However, Congress must exercise discipline regarding the money it borrows. We have provided this discipline by specifying a targeted guideline of 20 percent of Gross Domestic Product (GDP) with the power of Congress to override that guideline by a two-thirds vote of both Houses. We believe such limitation, in conjunction with Congress's obligation to make declarations with respect to its laws, will give Congress flexibility to borrow money if a super-majority consensus believes that to be in the best interests of the country.

The federal government spending as a percentage of GDP over the past fifty years is shown in the following chart:

Federal Outlays and Revenues, 1930 -2015 (as percentage of GDP)

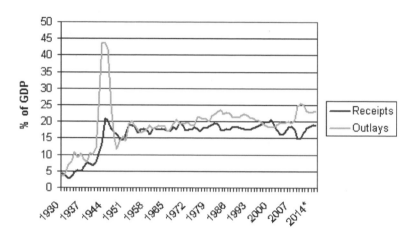

© 2010 National Priorities Project, Inc.

Source: *Budget of the United States Government, Fiscal Year 2011, Historical Table 1.2*

CONSTITUTIONAL LANGUAGE

Congress shall have no power to appropriate monies for any year for which a budget has been established by Congress of a sum greater than one-fifth of the Gross Domestic Product of the United States for the prior year as determined by Congress unless the appropriation is approved by a two-thirds vote of both Houses.

22

AMENDMENT NO. 30.10: NO SPECIAL BENEFITS

SUMMARY

30.10 Congress shall have no retirement, health, or other pension benefit law for itself or federal employees, except the military, unless the law applies to everyone.

COMMENT

We begin this amendment with the comment that the most important duty our federal government has under the Constitution is to provide for the general defense of this nation. Although the defense of the nation can take many forms, including diplomacy, the use of the military is the most important. Those who risk and lose their lives in the defense of our nation are entitled to be treated separately and provided with such benefits as Congress deems appropriate.

While the military is a special case, we see no reason that members of Congress or federal employees should have a special safety net because they work for the federal government. In most cases, their safety nets cost more than those available to workers in the private sector. The effect is to pass on costs to later generations to cover these safety nets for retired federal workers.

Proper pay-as-you-go business requires Congress to pay federal workers a fair wage with sufficient funds to defray any health or pension benefit they may wish to have and to make them subject to the same laws crafted by Congress to benefit all Americans.

As a matter of fairness, we have provided in Amendment 29.2 (Chapter 7) a method for dealing equitably with members of Congress and federal employees who have relied on existing law for their retirement. This method gives Congress two years from the adoption of this amendment to calculate the present value of the future benefits of these persons and to thereafter pay such persons in cash or over time as Congress shall determine.

CONSTITUTIONAL LANGUAGE

Congress shall have no power to pass any bill conferring a retirement, health, pension, or other benefit upon itself or its past, present, or future members or any employee of the United States or agency thereof, except the military, unless such bill applies generally to all other citizens.

23

AMENDMENT NO. 30.11:
NO PRESIDENTIAL SPENDING
AUTHORITY

SUMMARY

30.11 Congress shall not delegate spending authority to
the President.

COMMENT

Political gamesmanship played by the President and the Congress
offends the sensibilities of our citizens. Thus, for example, no senator
or congressman wants to be seen as voting to increase the debt limit
because, generally speaking, most Americans are against that. The
President argues for increases because the government cannot continue to operate without those increases and cites positions scaring
every person who is in any way connected directly or indirectly to
a government program. Congress, on the other hand, does not have
the courage to find the almost impossible solution to this problem.
Rather, Congress refuses to increase the debt limit unless it receives
concessions that it believes most people would find reasonable. We

can safely say that if Congress fixed this nation's spending problem, most of its members would not be reelected. The result is Congress will not fix the problem, preferring to rely on inflation to do its job and then blame someone else for the inflation.

This phenomenon occurred in 2011. The result was the Budget Control Act of 2011, which allowed the President to increase the debt by $1.2 trillion upon fifteen days' notice unless Congress objected. Since it would be impossible today to obtain a veto-proof resolution of objection, this allowed many senators and congressman to vote against the debt increase for political purposes back home without accepting responsibility for that debt increase. The Founding Fathers would never have allowed such a delegation of financial authority from the Congress to the President, and it should be prohibited in the future in order to make Congress responsible and accountable for the financial operations of this country. The other problem is that there is nothing citizens can do to challenge this unconstitutional delegation because the courts will say they have no standing. See Amendment 36.2 Commentary (Chapter 43). Further, it is likely unconstitutional for a majority of Congress to pass a law with a stipulation that the law can only be undone by a two-thirds vote.

The spending authority of our nation is one of the most solemn duties Congress has. Because of the Fourteenth Amendment, the United States is forbidden to dishonor "the validity of the public debt...authorized by law." Yet, Congress delegates to the executive branch (the Secretary of the Treasury) the authority to borrow money without Congressional approval, with the only discipline being the debt limit Congress has approved. The Secretary of the Treasury cannot borrow money in excess of this limit. Until 1917, Congress voted on each and every new issuance of debt and specified the amount and terms of the debt. We have not recommended that Congress renew the practice before 1917, believing tighter control over spending or the debt limit will be sufficient.

Whether Congress can delegate legislative authority to the President has been addressed by the Supreme Court. The general rule is that delegation is unconstitutional if there is a lack of standards in the duties conferred upon the executive agency. Thus, the search for adequate standards to restrict administrative discretion in the executive branch lies at the heart of every delegation challenge. The essential inquiry is whether the specified guidance "sufficiently marks the field within which the Administrator is to act so that it may be known whether he has kept within it in compliance with the legislative will." In this respect, the courts will look at the totality of the standards, definitions, contexts, and prior practices to see whether they provide an adequate intelligible principle to guide and confine administrative decision making.

The Supreme Court has stated that a constitutional power implies a power of delegation of authority sufficient to effect its purposes, that appropriation power is not functionally distinguishable from other powers that have been delegated by Congress, and that many delegations of authority have been recognized in the areas of immigration, federal crime, war, fixing prices for commodities and rents, determining when, if ever, a law should take effect, and others. The necessity of delegation is sometimes discussed, but there is no case finding an unconstitutional delegation based on a lack of necessity.

Illustrative of the problem is the Budget Control Act of 2011 discussed above, which is equivalent to contingent legislation. The contingency was that under certain circumstances the President could increase the debt limit by $1.2 trillion. We have no objection to reasonable and proper delegation of legislative authority to the executive branch and its agencies. However, the delegation of authority to increase the national debt by $1.2 trillion is believed by most people to be outside the circle of acceptable delegation. The sole purpose of the Budget Control Act of 2011 was to mislead the American people into believing that the issue of the size of the spending limit would be reconsidered by Congress and acted on in the usual manner. Yet, the legislation was really structured for political purposes, having nothing to do with the intelligent management of the nation but rather giving certain elected officials a chance to go on record against an increase when they were really for it.

The notion that the President can have authority subject to the disapproval of Congress is a legally unchallengeable act (except by a congressman). It is an unconstitutional trick essentially requiring a two-thirds vote (veto-proof act) to undo the debt increase even though our Constitution requires only a majority vote to pass the law.

CONSTITUTIONAL LANGUAGE

Congress shall have no power to pass any bill delegating to the President the authority to take any action subject to Congress's disapproval or to increase spending authority related to any government obligations the budget authority for which has not been provided in advance, unless such delegation is necessary and accompanied by clearly defined and ascertainable standards.

AMENDMENT NO. 31: TIMELY APPOINTMENTS

SUMMARY

31.0   The President and Senate shall act in a timely manner on the President's appointment of judges, ambassadors, and other public ministers or they shall not be paid.

COMMENT

The second paragraph of Article II § 2 of the Constitution gives the President the power to "nominate, and by and with the Advice and Consent of the Senate…appoint Ambassadors, other public Ministers and Consuls, Judges of the supreme Court, and all other Officers of the United States, whose Appointments are not herein otherwise provided for, and which shall be established by Law.…"

Both the President and the Senate manipulate this provision in the Constitution for political purposes. The President can allow vacancies on federal courts and elsewhere to remain pending a forthcoming election if he is concerned that the consent of the Senate will not be forthcoming. The Senate, on the other hand, pursuant to protocols among Senators, gives the Senator in whose State a particular person is to be appointed great influence as to whether that person is approved in committee or brought to the floor of the Senate for a vote. In addition, the Senate as a whole, if managed by a party different than that of the President, can delay appointments to achieve other political objectives.

As of 2008, when we last looked at this issue, 520 days elapsed on average for the Senate to deny consent to those federal district court judges nominated for appointment, an increase from 170 days in the late 1970s. Those persons who were favorably accepted increased to 182 days from approximately 70 days. These delays are outrageous because decent, honorable people who have committed to serve at the request of the President must put their lives on hold pending action by the Senate. In the meantime, important posts remain vacant, and the public's business is put at peril. On January 28, 2012, *The New York Times* in its lead editorial stated, "Filibustering Nominees Must End" and added:

> Changing the rule is a risky course, but the only way to get the nation's work done. The system for reviewing presidential appointments is broken. The Senate has a constitutional duty to provide advice and consent on the naming of judges and high-ranking executive branch officials. But the process has been hijacked by cynical partisanship and cheap tricks.
>
> This is not a new problem, but it has gotten intolerably worse and is now threatening to paralyze government, as Republicans use the filibuster to try to kill off agencies they do not like. The number of unfilled judicial seats is nearing a historic high.

It is time to end the ability of a single senator, or group of senators, to block the confirmation process by threatening a filibuster, which can be overcome only by the vote of 60 senators....[14]

We believe a sanction of eliminating compensation to all Senators and the President if they fail to take timely action under the proposed amendment is a sufficient impetus to compel obedience to constitutional duty. Under the proposed amendment, the President has ninety days from a vacancy to nominate a successor, and the Senate has 120 days thereafter to consent. Upon consent, the President has thirty days to make an appointment.

CONSTITUTIONAL LANGUAGE

The President shall nominate ambassadors, other public ministers and consuls, judges of the Supreme Court, and all other federal courts established by Congress upon the advice and consent of the Senate within ninety days of any vacancy, and the Senate shall confirm or reject such nomination within 120 days thereafter, whereupon, if the nomination is consented to, the President shall appoint the person so nominated within thirty days. If the President or the Senate, as the case may be, do not timely act, the compensation otherwise payable to the President or members of the Senate and its staff shall be abated without recoupment until such action is taken.

25

AMENDMENT NO. 32.1: PRIORITIZE AGENCIES

SUMMARY

32.1   The President shall prioritize all federal agencies with a number to resolve conflicts between agencies and preserve the rule of law.

COMMENT

One can easily discern that when there are thousands of regulations, there will be conflicts among the regulations of any single agency and conflicts between the regulations of one agency and any other agency. The courts have had occasion to deal with these conflicts. In 1985 the Federal Claim Court ruled that Department of Defense regulations prevailed over Army regulations. In 2009 that court ruled that Department of Defense regulations prevailed over inconsistent Air Force regulations.

Today, it is estimated that there are more than 1,300 distinct organizations across all three branches of the federal government. In all probability, the number of these agencies is growing and not diminishing. We publish so many regulations that it is more appropriate to gauge the number of them by referring to the pages. In 1970 the Code of Federal Regulations contained 54,834 pages. By 1998 the Code of Federal Regulations contained 134,723 pages (201 volumes). In 2008 ABC News reported that the pages in a single title of one volume, when removed and then attached end to end, rolled out the length of one and a half football fields. Another report in 2008 measured the linear width of these volumes at 304 inches. These numbers have continued to grow.

As one can imagine, many of these regulations impose penalties for noncompliance and generate a strong probability of conflict, established to be exponential by mathematical calculations. Currently, these conflicts, to the extent they are not resolved in a court proceeding, are resolved by people presumably trying to do the right thing. However, the notion that the law is ultimately determined by people is inconsistent with the notion of the rule of law and causes society to degenerate into the rule of men. When men begin to rule, freedom begins to die.

The proposed amendment requires the President to number each federal agency and thereafter provides that the agency with the lowest number prevails over agencies with larger numbers. The method of resolving conflict is simple and easy. The only remaining hurdle is the resolution of conflicting regulations within a particular agency. This the courts will have to resolve. Further, this process ensures that there is but one government ruling us and not a plethora of many governmental agencies exhibiting their power and imposing their rules upon ordinary Americans as their activities in some fashion fall under a particular agency and its regulations.

CONSTITUTIONAL LANGUAGE

All agencies of the federal government having the authority to issue regulations shall receive a priority number by the President by January 1 of each even-numbered year with the highest priority being the lowest number. Conflicts among valid regulations among agencies shall be resolved in favor of the agency having the highest priority. New agencies not having a priority number shall have the lowest priority in the order established unless the President amends his prior prioritization.

26

AMENDMENT NO. 32.2:
LIMIT AGENCY AUTHORITY

SUMMARY

32.2   Congress's delegation of legislative authority to federal agencies shall be strictly construed.

COMMENT

Under the Constitution, each of the branches of government is delegated power. In order to preserve the separation of powers, a concept essential to our freedoms, the Supreme Court has established that one branch cannot delegate its powers to another branch. In *Marshall Field & Co. v. Clark*, 143 U.S. 649 (1892), the Supreme Court said, "That Congress cannot delegate legislative power to the President is a principle universally recognized as vital to the integrity and maintenance of the system of government ordained by the Constitution." A general exception to the foregoing rule is that Congress can delegate regulatory authority to the President or executive agencies having legislative implications as long as standards are applied. However, over the years, the standards required to support this delegation have degenerated into standards such as the public interest. The only reason Congress would do this is because it is lazy and would prefer for the regulators to determine standards that should more appropriately be determined by Congress. The growth and breadth of federal agencies is a concern to everyone. A good way to restrain them is to require Congress to establish better standards and require courts to restrict agency powers in doubtful situations by strictly construing their authority. It is also appropriate that agencies that are, in effect, executing legislative power not have a privilege to withhold any information from Congress.

CONSTITUTIONAL LANGUAGE

The delegation of legislative power by Congress to the President or any department or any executive agency shall be accompanied by standards and shall be strictly construed. If there is any doubt concerning whether a government official has delegated power, the presumption shall be that he does not. Courts shall not defer to the judgment of legislative or executive officials with respect to their power nor accord to them any presumption of authority but shall require strict proof. Whether any regulation is authorized by law is at any trial a question of fact for the trier of fact, though the court can reverse a finding that authority exists if it believes as a matter of law there is no authority. No agency to which legislative power is delegated shall have any privilege to withhold information from Congress.

27

AMENDMENT NO. 32.3:
NO RETROACTIVE REGULATIONS

SUMMARY

32.3   Proposed agency regulations shall have no effect
until finally approved.

COMMENT

By proposed amendment 30.2 (Chapter 14), we have suggested that
the current authority of Congress to pass retroactive laws be limited
to bills passed by a two-thirds vote of both Houses. We also believe
agencies should not be allowed to pass retroactive regulations under
any circumstances except to correct mistakes in regulations that impose greater restrictions on the people than were intended.

Since most people do their planning on a yearly basis, it is fair
that they be able to know in advance what the laws will be for a particular year, most especially tax laws that have such a significant influence on economic planning. It stands to reason that, if Congress
wants to change the income tax laws in a particular year, it should
not make those laws effective until the first of the following year. Yet,
the Congress in enacting general revenue statutes has almost with-

out exception given such laws an effective date prior to the date of enactment. The Supreme Court has authorized this practice, holding that it does not violate due process if reasonable (*U.S. v. Darusmont,* 449 U.S. 292 (1981)). Our lives and decisions should not be made to depend on whether judges think retroactive tax laws are reasonable. The Supreme Court has also held that treasury regulations may be retroactively applied unless doing so constitutes an abuse of discretion (*Automobile Club of Michigan v. Commissioner,* 353 U.S. 180, 184 (1957)).

CONSTITUTIONAL LANGUAGE

Except to correct mistakes in regulations which impose greater restrictions on the people than were intended, proposed regulations made by any agency of the United States shall have no effect for any purpose whatsoever until they are adopted, and then their effect shall be prospective.

28

AMENDMENT NO. 32.4: NO MULTIPLE APPLICATIONS

SUMMARY

32.4   Applications for federal permits shall be made to one agency only and ruled upon promptly.

COMMENT

The process of creating wealth requires an idea, a committed individual, labor, and capital. The result is productivity, which creates wealth and in our system of government benefits everyone. We call this capitalism, namely the economic order that results from a free society. This order lets the market establish priorities and is based on a collective confidence that individuals whose fortunes are at risk are better suited to manage the capital than a government bureaucrat. The percentage of new ideas that are successful is low because there are many obstacles that retard the decision-making necessary for reaching a profitable result. Each decision involves a prediction about what will happen when a certain action is taken. Yet, no one, including the government, is an expert in making decisions, and, when they are wrong as determined by the marketplace, there is always failure and loss and injury to the people, with the number hurt depending on the level of government where the decision is made.

In order to stimulate the creation of wealth and the productivity essential to that end, it is in our interest to minimize the obstacles to a reasonable extent. Today, one of the most serious obstacles is the necessity as established by law and regulation that so many activities be approved in advance by governmental officials and permitted before they can take place. We have all heard about the Canadian pipeline, which has been seeking permits to install an oil pipeline from Canada to New Orleans and the numerous permits the owners were required to obtain from State and federal officials.

The federal government has a legitimate interest in requiring that some businesses file applications with it and receive permits to engage in the proposed activity. This is particularly true when public health and safety are affected in more than one State. However, placing the burden and risk on the applicant becomes an unfair burden on the creation of wealth when too many permits and too many government decision-makers are involved. In fact, substantial amounts of capital are required simply to obtain permission to engage in an activity that creates wealth, employment, and benefits for all of us.

In order to reverse a growing trend of excessive governmental interference with business activity, we have proposed that the federal government, in those areas where permits are required, manage its affairs in such a manner that an applicant need apply to one agency only. From that point, the particular agency is responsible for dealing with all of the interests of any other affected agency in such manner as it considers appropriate. In addition, we have proposed that this process not be extended and drawn out but resolved in a shorter time. We believe such a process will accelerate the creation of wealth and employment of our citizens and provide the benefits the applicant seeks to present to the people in exchange for a profit the applicant believes the people will find acceptable.

CONSTITUTIONAL LANGUAGE

No person shall be required to file an application to obtain a right or permit required by law with more than one agency or department, and that agency or department shall coordinate as it deems appropriate with other agencies and departments that have an interest in the matter. If more than one agency or department requires an application for permit, the applicant has the right to select which of the agencies or departments shall receive his application unless otherwise specified by law. Any such application shall be acted upon by the agency or department within one year from the filing thereof or shall thereafter be deemed unconditionally approved as filed. A denial, or approval with conditions that are not satisfied within six months from agency action from the applicant's submission of a satisfaction of conditions, shall be subject to judicial review before the federal court of appeals of the circuit in which the applicant resides.

John Adams, October 30,1735-July 4,1826

29

AMENDMENT NO. 32.5: PRESIDENT ANSWERS QUESTIONS

SUMMARY

32.5   Upon request of the House of Representatives, the
        President shall appear before it while in session to
        answer questions but not more often than weekly
        and for not more than forty minutes for each
        appearance.

COMMENT

The British do not have a written constitution, with the effect that they hold their democracy together through a changing and evolving set of procedures relating to decision-making generally. These procedures, being acceptable to people, become customs operating to balance competing tensions that exist in the management of people. One of these customs is the right of members of Parliament to question the Prime Minister for thirty minutes each Wednesday while Parliament is in session. The Parliament has established procedures that must be followed in terms of submitting questions so that the Prime Minister knows what to expect. It is a useful tool in many respects because it humbles the Prime Minister, makes the Prime Minister continuously aware he serves at the sufferance of Parliament, and forces the Prime Minister to deal with issues that he might prefer to avoid.

In contrast, the President of the United States, being the head of a separate branch of government, has no obligation to speak to Congress except to deliver State of the Union address, which has sometimes been delivered in writing. When the President does speak, it is usually at a press conference to reporters or in a meeting called by him attended by select congressmen or senators. This system tends to reinforce hubris, ignorance, and disinformation, on one hand, and diminish congressional leadership, truth, and clarity, on the other.

While it would be a radical shift for us Americans to adopt a British system entirely, a proposition many find more comforting than our own, we believe that requiring the President to answer to Congress upon its request for not more than forty minutes once a week while Congress is in session would be of great benefit to the people. For example, it has occurred to us that Congress could easily be equipped with electronic buttons wherein they could record their opinion as to whether the President was answering or avoiding the question. We all know that politicians love to skirt uncomfortable questions and talk about something else. Overall, the opportunity would be refreshing and helpful and is therefore recommended.

CONSTITUTIONAL LANGUAGE

Upon request of the House of Representatives, the President shall appear before it while in session to answer questions but not more often than weekly and for not more than forty minutes for each appearance.

30

Amendment No. 33.1: Constitutional Amendments by States

SUMMARY

33.1   A majority of State legislatures shall have the right to submit amendments to the Constitution to the States for ratification by three-fourths of the States.

COMMENT

Article V of the Constitution provides for two methods of changing the Constitution. The first method permits Congress to recommend changes to the States, which can then ratify those changes by a three-fourths majority vote of the States. The other method, relied upon by Campaign Constitution, is to permit two-thirds of the States to seek a Constitutional Convention to make changes to the Constitution. When two-thirds of the States agree, Congress must order a Constitutional Convention. Following the Constitutional Convention, Congress can refer the proposed changes to either the States for ratification by three-fourths thereof or for ratification by constitutional conventions in each of the States for ratification by three-fourths of such conventions.

The latter method is cumbersome. It has never been used before. It may be the only way we, the people, can take our country back and make the changes necessary to put our country on a solid footing. It would be appropriate to give the people a better, more efficient way of making changes to the Constitution other than those recommended by Congress.

For the above reasons, we propose this Amendment to allow the legislatures of the several States to propose amendments to the Constitution in the same fashion as Congress and, upon such proposals, such Amendments will be referred to the States for ratification by three-fourths of the States. When the Constitution was originally signed, such a procedure would have been impossible because of the methods of communication. However, with today's electronic systems of communication, this is a reasonable, viable, and feasible approach and gives the States a dignity equal to Congress when it comes to amending the Constitution.

This method is also facilitated by the establishment of a Board of Governors as set forth in proposed amendment 35.4 (Chapter 40), which will allow the States to work together to coordinate those actions that they, collectively, based upon the actions of their several legislatures, believe to be in the best interests of America.

CONSTITUTIONAL LANGUAGE

Whenever a majority of the legislatures of the several States propose amendments to this Constitution, they shall file the same with Congress, which shall within four months return the proposed amendments to the legislatures of the several States with such advice as it deems appropriate and, upon such return or upon the failure of Congress to timely make such return, the proposed amendments with Congress's return, if any, shall be submitted to the legislatures of the several States and, when ratified by the legislatures of three-fourths of the several States, the proposed amendments shall be valid to all intents and purposes according to the provisions thereof.

CHAPTER 31

AMENDMENT NO. 33.2: SAVE THE BILL OF RIGHTS

SUMMARY

33.2   Amendments to the Bill of Rights or to the Thirteenth, Fourteenth, and Fifteenth Amendments shall not be authorized without unanimous approval of all the States.

COMMENT

The demographics of America are changing. Emerging religious groups may find the First Amendment to be a restriction that they would prefer to avoid. They may also prefer to avoid other rights deemed important to Americans, which have not been touched since the founding of the country and which most people believe should never be touched. These rules that govern our society have the sanctity of the Magna Carta, and it seems appropriate that the only way to change them be by unanimous vote of the States.

CONSTITUTIONAL LANGUAGE

Any amendment changing the Bill of Rights or the Thirteenth, Fourteenth, or Fifteenth Amendments shall not be valid unless ratified by all the States.

AMENDMENT NO. 34.1: VOTING TAX

SUMMARY

34.1   As a condition to the right to vote in a federal election, every citizen shall annually pay an equal tax sufficient to raise revenues necessary to operate Congress, provided the tax shall begin at $10 and, when changed, shall never be more than the cost of one-fourth of one troy ounce of silver.

COMMENT

As shown in our Amendment 34.4 Commentary (Chapter 35), the current budget for operating Congress is about $4.5 billion per year. Although almost everyone pays a federal tax of some kind (e.g., gasoline tax), many pay no income tax, the revenue from which is intended to defray the general obligations of the federal government.

In order to evidence and confirm a responsible attachment to the affairs of Congress and the government and to eliminate voter fraud, we believe a modest and limited voting tax would be an appropriate condition to voting, notwithstanding the Twenty-Fourth

Amendment. The intent is to educate voters by conditioning their participation in government by some modest measure of cost, effort, and responsibility, which becomes a badge of honor. Even those who wanted to vote in ancient Greece had to get to the Pnyx before it filled up.

Is there any logic behind this tax? We know that a voter has to take the time to register to vote, which costs time and money. We know that it also costs a voter time and money to go to the polls and vote. We know that a voter pays sales and gasoline taxes in the ordinary course of affairs. However, in our view, he never participates in the actual administration of government unless he fills out a government form and pays a little money. The very act of doing this and paying one's share of the cost of running Congress reinforces a direct relationship between the voter and the government and highlights the understanding that what government does costs money. The process of filling out a form is education, which is bound to enhance participation in government and give us a more informed citizenry. The alternative is that we slowly delegate to others the power to decide for us, and their influence over our institutions changes them in ways that protects them from accountability. This has already happened. It is why Campaign Constitution was formed. One thing is certain: The current system is not working since the percentage of registered voters to eligible voters continues to fall. See Amendment 30.1 Commentary (Chapter 13). The only inference one can make is that a large portion of actual voters are influenced to vote, not by a concern for country, but by political influence to support or defeat a particular candidate. We anticipate much discussion on this proposal but believe the subject deserves debate whether or not it is finally included in changes to the Constitution approved by the States.

CONSTITUTIONAL LANGUAGE

Notwithstanding Amendment XXIV, as long as the United States obtains revenue under the Sixteenth Amendment, every citizen of the United States eighteen years or older shall file an income tax return and, notwithstanding any other law or provision of this Constitution, make a tax payment equal to the cost of operating Congress divided by the last census of the population of the United States rounded to the nearest dollar but not more than the cost of one-fourth troy ounce of silver nor less than ten dollars and, upon payment, shall receive evidence thereof, which evidence shall be shown as a condition to the right of such person to vote in any federal election. Such amount until changed by Congress shall be ten dollars and, when changed by Congress, shall be published by the President no later than the first business day after January 1 of each even-numbered year.

33

AMENDMENT NO. 34.2: LIMITED NUMBER OF REGULATIONS

SUMMARY

34.2   Federal regulations cannot exceed four times the size of federal statutes.

COMMENT

The number of federal laws and related regulations with which we must live seems to depend on the source. One report summarized the statements of various members of Congress, showing much disagreement on the subject. One thing is undisputed. There are too many. Title 26 of the Code of Federal Regulations (the part written by the Internal Revenue Service) contains 20 volumes, or 13,458 pages. At the same time, the Internal Revenue Code written by Congress contains 3,387 pages, meaning that the regulations were four times larger than the law in pages without adjustment for the size of the print.

One thing is clear, which is that the more laws and regulations we have, the less rule of law we have. Rule of law is a fundamental discipline essential to the continuation of democracy and freedom. We have all heard that the Affordable Care Act is 2,700 pages long and that the Dodd-Frank Wall Street Reform and Consumer Protection Act was close to that. Who do you suppose writes these laws? Who gives instructions to the secretaries in the back room about what to put in these laws? Who decides whether certain provisions should be included or left out? Or what provisions from other laws should be copied and pasted in? Who reads these laws? Why is it that after the Affordable Care Act was passed Congress immediately had to pass amendments containing hundreds of pages? Computers are handy, but they are used by Congress without discipline to give us runaway laws. If members of Congress had to write these laws themselves without the support of any staff, we can be sure they would be substantially shorter and restrain Congress from much of the complexity and cross-referencing it now uses.

One must also realize that in addition to regulations promulgated by agencies with the permission of Congress, those agencies in turn issue bulletins, executive directives, and other orders to facilitate the management of their mission.

We will let the voters put restraint on the amount of laws created by Congress but believe the number of regulations should not exceed in quantity some factor of those laws. Since the Internal Revenue regulations are considered some of the most complex we have and since the ratio was four to one in 2006, we believe the four times ratio is appropriate.

CONSTITUTIONAL LANGUAGE

The total size of all regulations issued by all agencies and departments of the United States, measured in bytes of text, shall not exceed four times those contained in all federal statutes, and any regulations in excess of such amount shall be void as of January 1 of each even-numbered year in the reverse order of the promulgating agency's priority. No later than November 1 of each odd-numbered year, Congress shall publish the bytes of text in all federal statutes effective for the following year, and the President shall publish the bytes of text in all regulations of all agencies by priority number for the following year.

George Washington, February 22,1732-Decemebr 14,1799

34

Amendment No. 34.3: Limited Life of Regulations

SUMMARY

34.3   Federal regulations shall automatically be void ten years after their adoption unless earlier approved by Congress for a stated term.

COMMENT

You are referred to proposed amendment 34.2 (Chapter 33) for a discussion of the problem of regulations. This amendment automatically voids regulations after ten years unless approved by Congress before then. The benefit of this provision is that federal regulators must be sensitive at all times to the regulations they have promulgated to manage whatever tasks Congress and the President have assigned to them. If they are important enough to continue after ten years, they will need congressional approval. Otherwise, the regulations will lapse.

We believe this discipline in the bureaucratic structure of the federal government is essential to preserve and maintain the rule of law and to discipline federal bureaucrats with sensitivity to the public that unimportant and unneeded regulations have a limited life.

CONSTITUTIONAL LANGUAGE

Regulations shall be void ten years after they are effective unless earlier approved by Congress for a stated term. Congress shall have the authority to exempt specified regulations from this provision.

35

AMENDMENT NO. 34.4: LIMIT NUMBER OF CONGRESSIONAL STAFF

SUMMARY

34.4   Congressional staff shall be limited to twenty-five thousand persons unless increased by a majority vote of the State legislatures upon the request of Congress.

COMMENT

In 2012 the expected budget for operating Congress, including all compensation payable to members of Congress and their staff, as well as the cost of its police force, buildings, the General Accounting Office, the congressional budget office, and others, is estimated to be $4.5 billion dollars. It is common knowledge that much of this money goes to compensate persons who support representatives and senators in their work both within their offices and in various committees. These persons are commonly referred to as "congressional staff." Some of these persons use their jobs as stepping stones to more rewarding opportunities requiring a knowledge of congressional operations and familiarity with particular persons who can make things happen. Others become experts and spend their professional years over complex laws like Social Security, Medicare, and the Internal Revenue Code. Without them, Congress in all likelihood would collapse.

In 2000 each congressman was entitled to fourteen staff persons, and each senator was entitled to thirty-four staff persons. Each House committee averaged sixty-eight persons, and each Senate committee averaged forty-six persons. We believe the size of staff over which any single elected representative can responsibly exercise supervision must be limited; otherwise, there comes a point when the staff begins to rule the nation. A single person has only so much time to manage activities where those activities involve the affairs of the nation. This is different from a chief executive officer, who manages a company with thousands of employees. In the latter case, those employees have intermediate managers each charged with a mission to accomplish some specific task, which is ultimately measured by the profit generated for the company.

Representatives in a democracy must continuously balance the needs of the public interest with the liberties and freedoms of individuals to ensure the preservation of that essential balance, which promotes creativity and provides incentives to work hard to better the lives of all.

The current staff numbers applicable in 2000 may or may not reflect what is appropriate to achieve this balance without losing control. Assuming that the relative ratios existing in 2000 between representatives and senators are appropriate, then one should know that at that time the House of Representatives was authorized to hire 6,090 people, and the Senate was authorized to hire 3,400 people, each without counting their committee staff. Other information shows that the Senate has twenty committees, seventy sub-committees, and four joint committees. The U.S. House of Representatives has twenty-three committees, of which three are special committees and twenty are standing committees, which are in turn divided into 104 sub-committees. One report states that in the 1990s, the House hired eleven thousand staff members, and the Senate hired six thousand staff members. It was recently reported that a large number of congressional staffers receive six-figure salaries, some as high as $163,000 per year. There are nearly two thousand House staffers with salaries of $172,500.

Since it is clear that the more staff members Congress has, the more work and laws they produce, it is also clear that, without proper limits, congressional staff will continue to grow and threaten our freedoms. As such, we believe that limiting the staff of Congress has the same discipline supporting the rule of law as does our proposed amendment limiting the number of regulations. We propose that the staff of representatives, senators, and the various committees not exceed twenty-five thousand persons. As a hedge against unforeseen demands, we recommend entrusting the State legislatures with the power to increase this number upon the request of Congress.

CONSTITUTIONAL LANGUAGE

Unless increased by a majority vote of the State legislatures upon the request of Congress, the total staff answerable to members of the House of Representatives and Senate and their committees shall not exceed twenty-five thousand persons for allocation among them as the members of Congress deem appropriate.

36

AMENDMENT NO. 34.5: UFO FULL DISCLOSURE

SUMMARY

34.5   No government person shall suppress information regarding UFOs.

COMMENT

The phenomena of unidentified flying objects and ancient cultures mystify Americans. In response to growing curiosity, the History Channel, the Discovery Channel, and others devote considerable time and money to displaying ancient information indicating that alien cultures previously existed on earth. Yet, few scholars and intellectuals either study or investigate the issue, and most of them reject the entire concept as fanciful. As with any phenomenon of this sort, there is usually a diehard minority who suspects a conspiracy that the government knows more than it is telling us and that this is wrong.

We believe that information, if any, related to unidentified flying objects or aliens should be disclosed to the American people. If, in fact, there is no such information, then the disclosure obligation is irrelevant. If there is such information, then there is no reason our government should know it and not the people since it would affect all of us.

We were influenced in proposing this amendment by the comments of Maurice Chatelain, a French mathematician and a specialist in radar radio transmissions, telecommunications, and orbital calculations. He began service in this country in our space program when he left France in 1955. In his book *Our Cosmic Ancestors* (1987), he made the following comments after describing the NASA space program in detail:

> But the astronauts were not limited to equipment troubles. They saw things during their missions that could not be discussed with anyone outside of NASA. It is very difficult to obtain any specific information from NASA, which still exercises a very strict control over any disclosure of these events.

> It seems that all Apollo and Gemini flights were followed, both at a distance and sometimes also quite closely, by space vehicles of extraterrestrial origin—flying saucers, or UFOs (unidentified flying objects), if you want to call them by that name. Every time it occurred, the astronauts informed Mission Control, who then ordered absolute silence.

> I think that Walter Schirra aboard Mercury 8 was the first of the astronauts to use the code name "Santa Claus" to indicate the presence of flying saucers next to space capsules. However, his announcements were barely noticed by the general public. It was a little different when James Lovell on board the Apollo 8 command module came out from behind the moon and said for everybody to hear: "We have been informed that Santa Claus does exist!" Even though

this happened on Christmas Day 1968, many people sensed a hidden meaning in those words that were not difficult to decipher.

James McDivitt was apparently the first to photograph an unidentified flying object, on 4 June 1965, when he was over Hawaii aboard Gemini 4. Frank Borman and James Lovell took magnificent photographs of two UFOs following Gemini 7 on 4 December 1965, at a distance of a few hundred yards. The UFOs looked like gigantic mushrooms with their propulsion systems clearly showing a glow on the underside.

The following year, on 12 November 1966, James Lovell and Edwin Aldrin in Gemini 12 also saw two UFOs at slightly over half a mile from the capsule. These were observed for quite some time and photographed repeatedly. The same happened to Frank Borman and James Lovell in Apollo 8 on Christmas Eve 1968, and to Thomas Stafford and John Young aboard Apollo 10 on 22 May 1969. The UFOs showed up both during the orbit around the Moon and on the homeward flight of Apollo 10.

Finally, when Apollo 11 made the first Moon landing on the Sea of Tranquility and, only moments before Armstrong stepped down the ladder to set foot on the Moon, two UFOs hovered overhead. Edwin Aldrin took several pictures of them. Some of these photographs have been published in the June 1975 issue of *Modern People* magazine. The magazine did not tell where it got them, vaguely hinting at some Japanese source.[15]

CONSTITUTIONAL LANGUAGE

No person in government, elected, hired, or appointed, shall suppress any information relating to the sighting or existence of extraterrestrial phenomena and shall have a duty to preserve and disclose any such information to the public promptly as it becomes available, including information existing at the time of the adoption of this amendment.

CHAPTER

37

AMENDMENT NO. 35.1: REINVIGORATE THE TENTH AMENDMENT

SUMMARY

35.1   The States or the people shall have all powers not delegated to Congress by the Constitution whether existing before or arising because of the Constitution.

COMMENT

In *U.S. Term Limits, Inc. v. Thornton*, 514 U.S. 779 (1995), the Supreme Court found that efforts by the States under the Tenth Amendment to limit the terms of their federal representatives were unconstitutional. The court adopted Justice Story's argument that the powers reserved could only be powers that existed before the Constitution and not powers springing out of the existence of the Constitution ("No state can say, that it has reserved, what it never possessed"). It is not likely the Founding Fathers even considered such a limitation to exist in the Constitution. We believe States should have all powers not delegated to the three branches of government by the Constitution and have therefore suggested this amendment.

CONSTITUTIONAL LANGUAGE

The powers not delegated to the United States by the Constitution, nor prohibited by it to the States, are reserved to the States respectively, or to the people. Such powers shall include all those powers not expressly delegated to Congress under the Constitution, whether or not those powers existed prior to the adoption of the Constitution or those arising thereafter as a result of the Constitution. The States shall not exercise these powers in a way that diminishes or interferes with the powers expressly delegated by the Constitution to Congress, the President, or the judiciary.

38

Amendment No. 35.2: Term Limits

SUMMARY

35.2   State legislatures shall have the power to limit the terms of members of Congress in their States.

COMMENT

In the 1980s there was much political discourse about whether our country could improve itself by limiting the terms of members of Congress. Congress itself did nothing. However, certain States determined that it would be better for them if their congressional members were exposed to term limits. Consequently, the legislatures in fourteen States passed term limit laws. Eventually, these laws were challenged and their constitutionality considered by the Supreme Court.

In *U.S. Term Limits, Inc. v. Thornton*, 514 U.S. 779 (1995), the Supreme Court held that the Tenth Amendment, by which powers not delegated to Congress were reserved to the States or the people, did not confer power on the States to adopt such legislation. The argument was the Tenth Amendment gave the States powers that existed prior to the Constitution but did not reserve to the States additional powers that arose by reason of the Constitution. See Amendment 35.1 Commentary (Chapter 37).

While the issue of term limits continues, sometimes with more intensity than at other times, we see no reason the States should not be able to limit the terms of their own federal representatives. In fact, we believe this is a far more preferable method of dealing with the issue than making a blanket rule applicable across the nation. The diversity of our many States permits the experimentation that, in the end, generates ideas that can be helpful to all of us. A general uniform rule, on the other hand, can result in mistake and stagnation. Moreover, it is much easier for a State to change its law on term limits than it is to change a constitutional amendment. It is also unlikely that members of Congress will ever impose term limits on themselves because there is a certain magic about Washington, D.C., that has a Sirenic appeal. In fact, one reads frequently about how long-term members of Congress, upon retirement, rather than go home where they came from, get a lobbying job or otherwise retire in Washington. The overall notion held by most Americans is that people have a duty to serve for a reasonable time to help their State and their country and are then expected to return and resume where they left off when their government service began.

CONSTITUTIONAL LANGUAGE

The legislature of each State shall have the power to limit the terms of the Senators and Representatives in Congress representing such State.

39

AMENDMENT No. 35.3:
STATE REPEAL OF FEDERAL LAWS

SUMMARY

35.3 Two-thirds of the State legislatures have the power to repeal a federal law.

COMMENT

Some scholars believe that States should have a right to repeal federal laws. The Constitution was ratified on the premise that the federal government would have limited powers and that the States and the people would have all other powers. Notwithstanding this intent, over the years the States have been limited largely to the exercise of police powers, with no say or very little in the management of the federal government.

This management was indirectly provided for in the Constitution as originally adopted, which provided that the State legislatures would elect U.S. Senators. However, fraud and corruption in State legislatures at the turn of the twentieth century gave rise to the progressive era, which presumed that the people were better qualified to decide who their U.S. Senators should be than their legislatures. The result was the Seventeenth Amendment, which was passed in 1913.

Over the years, persons elected to the U.S. Senate came to envision themselves as future presidents and rarely consulted their State legislatures with respect to material legislation.

While the Seventeenth Amendment is proposed for repeal by our proposed amendment 36.5 (Chapter 46), in an effort to increase the power of State legislatures and the accountability of the federal government and to improve the quality of leaders in the United States Senate, we have also deemed it important to enlarge the power of the States to allow their leaders to contribute to national policy by having veto authority over federal legislation.

Benefits of diversity within the States and the experimentation they can undertake cannot be overestimated. They are a valuable resource in the management of government and are largely unused in the management of the federal government. In order to give States a greater influence in the formulation of national policy, we believe it important to increase their powers and to provide a sort of *in terrorem* effect on any Congress that chooses to ignore them.

In order to give the States the necessary influence they deserve, we have suggested that they have the power to repeal federal law or remove federal judges by resolutions passed by two-thirds of the States. In order to do this, the States need a vehicle whereby their governors can convene to develop uniform issues and proposals and present them to their State legislatures. Currently, no such system is available, with the effect that the nation generally is denied the benefits of many knowledgeable, intelligent, and serious leaders.

CONSTITUTIONAL LANGUAGE

The legislatures of two-thirds of the several States shall have the power to repeal any law or part thereof or regulation of the United States or remove any federal judge or justice of the Supreme Court by a resolution describing the law or part thereof or regulation to be repealed or judge or justice to be removed with the effective date of such action being as stated in the resolution or upon obtaining the required approval, whichever date is later. Upon the required approval, the resolution shall be signed by the governors of the States having the approving legislatures, shall contain a certification of approval, and shall be delivered to the President and Congress by the governor last to sign and shall take effect as provided therein.

40

AMENDMENT NO. 35.4:
BOARD OF GOVERNORS

SUMMARY

35.4   There shall exist a Board of Governors (State governors) to assist States in the exercise of their powers under the Constitution.

COMMENT

Our effort to enhance the power of the States requires a method of exercising that power. We have chosen to do this by establishing a Board of Governors, which shall be authorized to meet as it sees fit according to rules it promulgates and to make decisions of national importance. Under the proposed amendment, governors cannot exercise their constitutional powers without the approval of their legislatures. The mere existence of this Board will act as a restraint on Congress and the President because of the Board's potential to critique congressional and national policy and educate citizens.

Of the forty-four proposed amendments initially suggested by us, six of them involve States, including the power to initiate amendments to the Constitution (Amendment 33.1, Chapter 30), the power to increase congressional staff (Amendment 34.4, Chapter 35), those additional powers conferred by clarification of the Tenth Amendment (Amendment 35.1, Chapter 37), the power to limit the terms of congressional members (Amendment 35.2, Chapter 38), the power to repeal federal laws (Amendment 35.3, Chapter 39), and the power to elect U. S. Senators as first envisioned by the Founding Fathers (Amendment 36.5, Chapter 46).

CONSTITUTIONAL LANGUAGE

There is hereby established a Board of Governors whose members shall be the governors of the several States, which shall act according to rules adopted by the governors of the several States. The Board of Governors shall have power by a two-thirds vote of its members to make recommendations to Congress or to their State legislatures and to administer all activities assigned to the States or State legislatures herein as they deem in the best interests of the United States. The Board of Governors shall be immune from all taxes.

41

Amendment No. 35.5: Legislatures Defined

SUMMARY

35.5 Approval by each State legislature means majority approval by all members of each House in the State's legislative branch.

COMMENT

This amendment is solely for the purpose of clarifying that a majority of both Houses of any State legislature is required for legislative approval and that such approval is of the whole number of legislators in each House and not a majority of a quorum.

CONSTITUTIONAL LANGUAGE

Any approval by the legislatures of the States as used in the Constitution means approval by a majority of all members of each House in their legislative branch.

42

AMENDMENT NO. 36.1: JURY DECIDES UNREASONABLENESS OF GOVERNMENT ACTION

SUMMARY

36.1   Whether any law is unconstitutional as applied (i.e., arbitrary and unreasonable under the circumstances) is a question of fact for a jury.

COMMENT

The Fifth Amendment to the Constitution states that "No person shall…be deprived of life, liberty, or property, without due process of law.…" The Fourteenth Amendment to the Constitution states, "nor shall any state deprive any person of life, liberty, or property, without due process of law.…" The term "due process" is defined by the courts to require fundamental fairness both in terms of the procedures utilized to take life, liberty, or property and the substance of the action, which is referred to as "substantive due process." Thus, regardless of the procedures used to implement any kind of taking, government actions that are fundamentally unfair are also barred

(*County of Sacramento v. Lewis*, 523 U.S. 833 (1998)). In the above case, the Supreme Court said:

> Since the time of our early explanation of due process, we have understood the core of the concept to be protection against arbitrary action....
>
> The principal and true meaning of the phrase has never been more tersely or accurately stated than by Mr. Justice Johnson, in *Bank of Colombia* v. *Okely*, 4 L. Ed. 559 (1819): "As to the words from Magna Charta, incorporated into the Constitution of Maryland, after volumes spoken and written with a view to their exposition, the good sense of mankind has at last settled down to this: that they were intended to secure the individual from the arbitrary exercise of the powers of government, unrestrained by the established principles of private right and distributive justice."
>
> We have emphasized time and again that "[t]he touchstone of due process is protection of the individual against arbitrary action of government...."

It is elsewhere said that a law is unconstitutional as applied if, in its application to specific circumstances, the action is deemed arbitrary. Thus, the constitutionality of the particular action cannot be determined by simply reading a law but can only be determined by considering the manner in which the law is applied and administered to a particular individual.

Currently, whether a law is unconstitutional as applied, that is whether governmental action is arbitrary, capricious and unreasonable, or violates fundamental fairness, is a question of law for the courts. We believe courts are no better suited to make this determination than a jury. We believe whether a government action is arbitrary and capricious should be decided by the jury in those cases where there is a jury. As added protection, we believe, if a jury should for some reason find that a given action was constitutional as applied, that the court should be able to reverse this finding based upon its view that the law was unconstitutional as applied. However, the court could never reverse a finding by the jury that the governmental action was unconstitutional as applied and determine it to be constitutional as applied.

We have to remember that one reason Hitler came to power was that he corrupted the judicial branch. Although we might think this a remote possibility here, it is nonetheless a possibility in any country, and it seems to us a hallmark for the protection of freedom to let juries decide what is reasonable and unreasonable. In fact, we believe this amendment may be the most important of all amendments proposed.

CONSTITUTIONAL LANGUAGE

Whether any law or regulation is unconstitutional as applied to particular circumstances is a question of fact for the trier of fact, though the court can reverse a finding by a jury of constitutionality as applied if it believes the law is unconstitutional as applied.

CHAPTER

43

AMENDMENT NO. 36.2: MORE CITIZEN STANDING

SUMMARY

36.2   Every citizen shall have standing in court to seek
the meaning of the Constitution or to challenge
the constitutionality or validity of any federal
law or regulation or to seek a declaration of the
meaning thereof.

COMMENT

Article III §1 of the Constitution states that "The judicial power of
the United States, shall be vested in one supreme Court, and in such
inferior Courts as the Congress may from time to time ordain and
establish." While this judicial power is vested in Article III §1, by
Article III §2, it "shall extend to all Cases...arising under this Constitution" and other "Controversies." The meaning of a "Case" has
occupied many court decisions with enough evolution and change
and dissenting opinions to muddle the clear meaning of that term.
Some decisions say, if there is no "Case," then there is no jurisdiction,
whereas others say, if there is no "Case," then there is no standing.

In either event, when a controversy is determined not to be a "Case," the courts will not hear the matter.

When a person believes there is some illegality in America and decides to do something in court, he has to have "standing." The first thing he notices is the language in *Marbury v. Madison*, 5 U.S. 137 (1803), that there is no standing unless there is "injury." Yet, the Supreme Court has made clear that not every injury will entitle one to standing and the protection of the laws. The Supreme Court has said one needs a particular kind of injury or he does not have standing. In *Baker v. Carr* 369 U.S. 186 (1962) (the "one man, one vote" case), the Supreme Court said there was standing when there was an actual controversy and the plaintiff alleged "a personal stake in the outcome of the controversy as to assure that concrete adverseness which sharpens the presentation of issues…." However, these simple rules began to change. In *Allen v. Wright*, 468 U.S. 737 (1984), the Supreme Court said standing was one of those doctrines that cluster about Article III, which "relate in part, and in different though overlapping ways, to an idea, which is more than an intuition but less than a rigorous and explicit theory, about the constitutional and prudential limits to the powers of an unelected, unrepresentative judiciary in our kind of government." Make sense? In its effort to give substance to the word, the Supreme Court has relied on tradition and a "concern about the proper—and properly limited—role of the courts in a democratic society" (*Warth v. Seldin*, 422 U.S. 490 (1975)), or "the idea of separation of powers" (*Allen v. Wright*). In *Allen v. Wright*, the court acknowledged the "absence of precise definitions" but stated it "hardly leaves courts at sea in applying the law of standing" as it proceeded to ask rhetorical questions that could only be answered by subjective determinations. The abyss of subjectivity is also made apparent by the lack of unanimity in the court on major standing questions, with dissenting justices complaining that standing decisions reflect a hostility to the underlying claims.

In an effort to give shape to an amorphous term, the court decided that the "central mechanism of separation of powers depends largely upon *common understanding* of what activities are *appropriate* to legislatures, to executives, and to courts" (emphasis supplied), *Lujan v. Defenders of Wildlife*, 504 U.S. 555, 559-560 (1992). In *Steel Co. v. Citizens for a Better Environment*, 523 U.S. 83, 102 (1998), the court stated, "standing to sue is part of the common understanding of what it takes to make a justiciable case." The court fails to define what is "appropriate" or what is a "common understanding." Complicating the matter is the court's position that the standing inquiry involves both constitutional and prudential limitations, the former dealing with jurisdiction itself and the latter dealing with the exercise of that jurisdiction. With respect to the former, the Supreme Court says, "Standing imports justiciability: whether the plaintiff has made out a 'case or controversy' between himself and the defendant within the meaning of Article III" (*Warth v. Seldin*, 422 U.S. at 498). Of course, the average person recognizes that these complicated and intertwined concepts give the courts wiggle room in avoiding cases they subjectively believe should not be decided.

Shackled by standing rules that did not always work, the court has crafted exceptions, a discussion of which is beyond the scope of this commentary. These exceptions relate to First Amendment cases or cases grounded in "weighty, countervailing policies" or cases involving public safety.

A review of the cases shows that, with the exception of *Baker v. Carr*, 369 U.S. 186 (1962), the Supreme Court's foray into a search for standards has not been helpful, as shown by the many exceptions, the controversies among the justices, the tendency of the Court to find standing when it wants to, and the definition of standing in terms of "tradition" or "the idea of democracy" or "the separation of powers" or "common understanding." The Supreme Court admits that standing "incorporates concepts concededly not susceptible of precise definition" and is characterized by the "absence of precise definitions." None of this bodes well for the rule of law.

It is time to put this issue to rest and require the Supreme Court or lower federal courts to hear cases even when they would prefer not to. If citizens cannot challenge the constitutionality or legality of federal laws, they have no way of enforcing accountability in the President or Congress.

CONSTITUTIONAL LANGUAGE

Every citizen shall have standing in court to seek a declaration of the meaning of any part of the Constitution or to challenge the constitutionality or validity of any federal law or regulation or to seek the meaning thereof.

AMENDMENT NO. 36.3:
MENS REA REQUIRED

SUMMARY

36.3   No person shall be guilty of a federal crime unless the person's *mens rea* has been proved beyond a reasonable doubt.

COMMENT

The term *mens rea* is Latin for "guilty mind." The due process requirement in American jurisprudence has always required some type of fault in addition to the particular action causing a crime. However, there is a growing body of strict liability crimes that result in penalties and punishment for which a guilty mind need not be proved. This trend adversely affects our freedoms as more and more federal crimes are passed. Since 2000, Congress has created at least 452 additional crimes. By 2007, the total number of federal crimes exceeded 4,450.

One experienced criminal attorney has stated:

…there are just too many federal crimes, many created by regulator fiat or otherwise without meaningful oversight by elected officials. [I am concerned] about how a great many of them are apparently drafted by people with no understanding of how criminal law works and why. About how, as a result, there are an insane number of federal crimes (all felonies, of course) that penalize without any *mens rea* requirement at all. The most innocent accident, the most harmless and unintentional error, can make any honest and decent citizen a felon.[16]

The growing trend to permit crimes without establishing *mens rea* opens the door to a tyrannical government. One can envision a situation in which a particular bureaucrat develops a negative animus against a citizen and then charges him with violation of numerous regulations imposing criminal penalties. There are circumstances in which the person did not have any idea he was doing anything wrong. It is one thing to assess a person civil damages for harm to the public occasioned by his actions, but it is another thing to label him a criminal, imprint that upon his public record, and make him the scourge of society when he did not know he was doing anything wrong.

The concept of *mens rea* has received its fair share of attention from legal scholars. Some have said that *mens rea* contains two factors: an actual harm (a social disvalue) and the mental state of the actor who commits the harm. These scholars disagree on whether the harmful act need imply immorality and whether a harmful act committed with laudable motives could be a crime. Oliver Wendell Holmes said, "It is quite futile to seek to discover the meaning of *mens rea* by any common principle of universal application...."[17] Since motive has no easy definition, its involvement in *mens rea* prevents formulation of a common principle essential to legality.

The courts will be challenged by this amendment as they attempt to formulate the mental elements essential to crimes and the requirement of "guilt." However, attention to this concept by the federal government is essential to our freedom. The States may depart from the standard subject to limitations of the Constitution.

It is not above the government to avoid the *mens rea* requirement. Thus, there are some cases where, for example, a federal prosecutor has argued that he did not have to prove "knowingly" when the person was charged with illegal "acquires" where the crime was "knowingly uses, transfers, acquires, alters, or possesses…[an illegal drug]." The reason: The term "knowingly" applied only to the term "uses" and not to other terms. The mere fact that the government would make such an argument establishes its proclivity to seek recognition for convictions regardless of the justice thereof. Today, where a criminal statute is silent as to *mens rea*, the courts will require proof of general intent ("general intent" means you knew you were committing the act complained of even though you did not know it was wrong to do so). The courts will enforce a criminal statute without *mens rea* if Congress so requires.

In the interest of protecting the freedom of individuals, we deem it important that *mens rea* be required as an element of proof in any federal crime.

CONSTITUTIONAL LANGUAGE

No person shall be guilty of a federal crime unless the person's *mens rea* has been proved beyond a reasonable doubt.

Benjamin Franklin, January 17, 1706-April 17,1790

45

Amendment No. 36.4: No Severance Clause

SUMMARY

36.4   If any part of a bill that becomes law is determined to be unconstitutional, the whole law shall be unconstitutional.

COMMENT

It is common practice for both lawyers and legislatures to put a "savings clause" in contracts and statutes to the effect that if any portion of the document is determined to be invalid, then the balance of the document shall continue to be valid. The result is that courts are left to enforce the document, even though some portion of it was determined to be invalid. This, in turn, causes one to wonder whether the document would ever have been approved in the first instance if the portion that was later established to be invalid had not earlier been included. Of course, this practice obscures what the real intention of the parties was.

    In order to promote and encourage responsibility in the drafting and approval of legislation, we believe the law should be that, if any portion of the legislation is later determined to be unconstitutional, the entire legislation shall be deemed invalid. This requires that Congress act responsibly and not clutter its legislation with risky features. These features should be included in separate legislation or separate laws.

Many will be reminded of certain discussions regarding the Affordable Care Act related to whether the entire law is unconstitutional if the individual mandate portion is unconstitutional. This is an issue the Supreme Court will have to deal with if it rules that the individual mandate is unconstitutional.

Overall, we believe this proposed amendment will make Congress more responsible and diligent in passing laws and will eliminate the inclusion in otherwise worthy legislation of provisions that, if found to be invalid, would invalidate the entire legislation.

CONSTITUTIONAL LANGUAGE

If any part of a bill that becomes law is determined to be unconstitutional, then the whole law shall be unconstitutional.

CHAPTER 46

AMENDMENT NO. 36.5: STATE LEGISLATURES ELECT U.S. SENATORS

SUMMARY

36.5   The Seventeenth Amendment to the Constitution requiring the direct election of Senators shall be repealed.

COMMENT

The Constitution as originally established provided that "The sum of the United States shall be composed of two Senators from each State, chosen by the legislature thereof, for six years, and each Senator shall have one vote." In 1913 the Seventeenth Amendment was adopted to provide for the direct election of Senators by the people. The result was that the States lost their influence over national policy, became similar to bureaucratic agencies so far as the Congress was concerned, and provided a platform for U.S. Senators to spend their time trying to become the President.

Unfortunately, fraud and corruption in State legislatures at the turn of the twentieth century gave rise to the progressive era, which presumed that the people were better qualified to decide on who their U.S. Senators should be than their legislators. The result was the Seventeenth Amendment, which was passed in 1913. Over the years, persons elected to the U.S. Senate came to envision themselves as future presidents and rarely consulted their State legislatures with respect to material legislation.

Repeal of the Seventeenth Amendment will increase the power of State legislatures, enhance the accountability of the federal government, improve the quality of leaders in the United States Senate, and allow State leaders to contribute to national policy.

The advantage of returning to the original constitutional intent would be to energize State legislatures and the members thereof, minimize campaigns for the U. S. Senate, minimize the cost of campaigns for the U. S. Senate, familiarize State legislatures with federal issues during the campaign of different persons to seek election from those legislatures, provide incentive to voters to pay more attention to who their State legislators are, and generate persons who will be recognized for their leadership and soundness of policy rather than their rhetoric and media appeal.

CONSTITUTIONAL LANGUAGE

The Seventeenth Amendment to the Constitution is repealed.

47

AMENDMENT NO. 36.6: LIMIT CONGRESSIONAL POWER

SUMMARY

36.6 The "general Welfare" clause as used in the preamble of the Constitution does not grant Congress any power and as used in Article I § 8 grants power exercisable only by at least a two-thirds vote of both Houses.

COMMENT

The term "general Welfare" is used in Article I § 8 cl. 1, which states, "The Congress shall have Power To lay and collect Taxes, Duties, Imposts and Excises, to pay the Debts and provide for the common Defence and general Welfare of the United States...." In *U.S. v. Butler*, 297 U.S. 1 (Jan. 6, 1936), the Supreme Court ruled that the "general Welfare" clause as so used gave the Congress more powers than were expressly enumerated in the Constitution. In *Helvering v. Davis*, 301 U.S. 619 (1937), the Supreme Court said:

> Congress may spend money in aid of the "general welfare." Constitution, Art. I, section 8; *United States v. Butler*, 297

U.S. 1 (1936) There have been great statesmen in our history who have stood for other views. We will not resurrect the contest. It is now settled by decision. *United States v. Butler, supra.* The conception of the spending power advocated by Hamilton and strongly reinforced by Story has prevailed over that of Madison, which has not been lacking in adherents. Yet difficulties are left when the power is conceded. The line must still be drawn between one welfare and another, between particular and general. Where this shall be placed cannot be known through a formula in advance of the event. There is a middle ground, or certainly a penumbra, in which discretion is at large. The discretion, however, is not confided to the courts. The discretion belongs to Congress, unless the choice is clearly wrong, a display of arbitrary power, not an exercise of judgment. This is now familiar law. "When such a contention comes here, we naturally require a showing that by no reasonable possibility can the challenged legislation fall within the wide range of discretion permitted to the Congress." [citations omitted] Nor is the concept of the general welfare static. Needs that were narrow or parochial a century ago may be interwoven in our day with the well-being of the nation. What is critical or urgent changes with the times.

The purge of nation-wide calamity that began in 1929 has taught us many lessons. Not the least is the solidarity of interests that may once have seemed to be divided....

While the decision in *U.S. v. Butler* was a loss to the strict constructionists, we believe it is unwise to trust a divided Congress with discretion over which specific programs are deemed to be for the common benefit or general welfare of the nation. To ensure that discretion is exercised with as much unanimity as is reasonable, we have recommended a two-thirds vote.

The desire to find more power in Congress than was intended by the Founding Fathers is illustrated by efforts to interpret the "general Welfare" clause in the Preamble of the Constitution as providing such power. The Preamble of the Constitution states, "We the People of the United States, in Order to form a more perfect Union, establish Justice, insure domestic Tranquility, provide for the common defence, promote the general Welfare, and secure the Blessings of Liberty to ourselves and our Posterity, do ordain and establish this Constitution for the United States of America." In *Carter v. Carter Coal Co.*, 298 U.S. 238 (May 18, 1936), four months after the *Butler* decision, the Supreme Court held that the "general Welfare" clause in the Preamble made no grant of authority to Congress to legislate substantively for the general welfare "and no such authority exists, save as the general welfare may be promoted by the exercise of the powers which are granted." The court also noted that the contrary position "often advanced and as often discredited" had no merit.

We believe a different court at a different time might change its interpretation of the Constitution. To ensure this does not happen, we believe it needs to be made clear that the "often advanced" argument that the "general Welfare" clause in the Preamble confers power on Congress can never be accepted. We have reason for this concern based on what the Supreme Court did with the "general Welfare" clause in Article I of the Constitution.

CONSTITUTIONAL LANGUAGE

The "general Welfare" as used in the Preamble of the Constitution refers to the whole of the American people and does not grant Congress any power with respect to any class of People. Congress shall have no discretionary power to spend money in aid of the "general Welfare" as used in Article I § 8 cl. 1 of the Constitution pursuant to a power not expressly enumerated in the Constitution, unless its action is approved by a two-thirds vote of both Houses.

48

AMENDMENT NO. 36.7: LIMIT EXECUTIVE PRIVILEGE

SUMMARY

36.7   Doubts as to whether the President can lawfully assert executive privilege on any matter to avoid releasing information to Congress shall be resolved against the President.

COMMENT

Clashes between the President and Congress are expected and have occurred frequently over the years when the President chooses not to release information that Congress would like released either to manage the country better or to embarrass the President. Any President with knowledge of this amendment would likely think twice about doing things that he would not want to be disclosed.

The availability of information is critical to the proper operation of a democracy. This amendment generally provides the courts with guidance in dealing with any issues that might be litigated to provide that, if there is a doubt as to whether the President has an executive privilege, the doubt shall be resolved against the President. In other words, in doubtful situations involving executive privilege, the President must disclose information.

CONSTITUTIONAL LANGUAGE

Doubts as to whether the President can lawfully assert executive privilege on any matter to avoid releasing information to Congress shall be resolved against the President.

PART 3

ESSAYS

49

ESSAY 1: REFORMING THE CONSTITUTION

The United States is a republic because the Founding Fathers recognized that it was the undisciplined passions of Athenian democracy that led to its downfall. To prevent this, they divided the powers of the federal government into three branches and honored local government by preserving the States. They also assumed that future leaders of our government would be as honorable as themselves. Madison said in *Federalist No. 55*:

> As there is a degree of depravity in mankind which requires a certain degree of circumspection and distrust, so there are other qualities in human nature which justify a certain portion of esteem and confidence. Republican government presupposes the existence of these qualities in a higher degree than any other form.[18]

They did not anticipate the cataclysmic changes of agriculture, the industrial revolution, the availability of cheap energy, or information and other technological changes that have occurred since 1787. More importantly, they did not anticipate the decline in the character of our leaders, who have subverted the principles of republican government by responding to the passions of a democratic populace willing to mortgage their children's future to enjoy benefits they need not pay for today. Hamilton in *Federalist No. 1* said:

> ...it will be equally forgotten that the vigor of government is essential to the security of liberty; that, in the contemplation of a sound and well-informed judgment, their interests can never be separated; and that a dangerous ambition more often lurks behind the specious mask of zeal for the rights of the people than under the forbidding appearance of zeal for the firmness and efficiency of government. History will teach us that the former has been found a much more certain road to the introduction of despotism than the latter, and that of those men who have overturned the liberties of republics, the greatest number have begun their career by paying an obsequious court to the people, commencing demagogues and ending tyrants.[19]

These changes created great wealth for America, which in turn influenced the growing power of politicians at the expense of the wisdom of statesmen. The competition for power between our major political parties has resulted in (1) an entitlement mentality with consequent increasing public expectations that entitlements are rights and not charity, (2) a shift in monetary obligations to the States without their consent, (3) an ill-advised reliance on polls, which poorly reflects the proper balance between short- and long-term national interests, (4) the utilization of tax policy, earmarks, and entitlement programs to enhance political power, (5) a willingness to favor elected representatives in Congress with benefits at public expense not available to others, (6) a delegation of undisciplined powers to regulatory agencies, (7) a disinterest in the impact laws have on freedom, (8) a disregard for the weakness of general planning, (9) a misplaced confidence in the reliability of economic planning, and (10) a disregard of the fundamental principle that wealth is created by freedom and the industry and creativity it inspires, without which we are unable to help those who cannot help themselves.

To rectify these changes and curb the unhealthy growth of government power, we have recommended process changes to the Constitution.

50

ESSAY 2: CHANGES TO THE CONSTITUTION

How does one decide whether the Constitution should be changed? Each of us has received emails or read published accounts over the years of suggested changes. I have considered all of those I have received over the past thirty years and included most of them in our proposals.

Our proposed changes are not necessarily ironclad. Our goal is to have changes that most people support. Our intent is to protect our republic and discourage tyranny. Once we select our organization leaders for the various States, we will find out soon enough whether some of these changes should go by the wayside or not. Our intent is that the proposed changes, if adopted, generate leaders who will do something about the currently existing disagreeable conditions in our country.

Many people are concerned that a constitutional convention would open the Constitution to all sorts of unacceptable changes. As a guard against this, we have asked the States to adopt a resolution that limits the desired constitutional convention to the issues in the resolution and that invalidates any effort to exceed the boundaries established by the resolution. See the Constitutional Convention Resolution.

In addition to the changes we have proposed, there are many other areas of American life influenced by the federal government that many people would prefer to see changed. However, amending the Constitution is not a panacea to restore the character of our nation. Some other changes have been mentioned from time to time and deserve consideration but are not included here, such as:

- The problem of high government salaries compared to salaries of private workers.
- The interminably long presidential campaigns.
- The lack of a draft of young people for military or public service.
- A deferential attitude toward certain Muslim practices in the United States.
- Federal government opposition to the exercise of State power to enforce federal law to protect State citizens.
- The conditions necessary to allow aliens to remain in the United States and become lawful citizens, including items such as filing federal tax returns, whether required or not (which tests their sense of responsibility and allows the government to keep track of them and their families), identification cards, no criminal backgrounds, no health issues, a deadline for speaking English, a test on the Constitution, and citizen sponsors.
- The issues of marriage and right to life.
- The extent to which English should be the formal and exclusive language of the nation.
- Whether the government should be able to condemn property for a private purpose.

- Except in special cases clearly involving interstate commerce, whether EPA authority should be limited to making recommendations without having enforcement authority.
- Whether a quasi-parliamentary system should be adopted, which would allow Congress to force a vote of confidence in and potentially remove the President.

We believe the changes we have proposed will result in the election of leaders who will responsibly deal with the above issues and other concerns the people have without making changes to the Constitution.

51

ESSAY 3:
PROCESS AMENDMENTS

We have elected to call the proposed changes to the Constitution presented by us "Process Amendments" because they largely affect the process by which decisions are made by Congress, the President, the States, and the people. Although our Process Amendments largely affect Congress and the President, they also affect the people and the States.

Congress. Thus, with respect to Congress, we have modified the concept of majority rule in order to promote harmony among elected representatives to achieve common solutions to national problems. We have imposed restrictions that prevent them from preferring themselves over citizens generally. We have required that they be responsible and make timely decisions in appropriate cases.

President. With respect to the President, we have given him the line-item veto but disciplined his management of federal agencies and required more transparency.

States. We have increased the power of the States, which has been diminished over the years to the status of administrative agencies. Each of our States has intelligent, educated, and commendable leaders who have as much or more knowledge and insight regarding human affairs as those elected to Congress. Yet, they have very little incentive to use the skills they have because of the ineffectual powers of the States and the restrictions imposed by Congress.

Voters. The people are the voters and have supreme power under the Constitution. We have imposed a minor burden on voters for the purpose of enhancing citizen responsibility. They will be required to pay a modest tax, costing less than three gallons of gas a year, as a condition to the right to vote in federal elections. We have proposed that the election of Senators be returned to State legislatures as originally required by the Founding Fathers. We have asked them to support their State legislatures to accept the changes we have proposed and to seek a Constitutional Convention.

Summary. In sum, we have placed a small burden on voting citizens, we have enlarged the powers of the States, and we have restricted the decision-making rights of Congress and the President to require responsibility, to impose harmony in dealing with each other, to enhance freedom, and to ensure a common reverence for the magical quality of a free people.

52

ESSAY 4:
FIRST PRINCIPLES

Freedom. The first principle of America is freedom—the core value of American culture. It explains why our little country in 1787, compared to larger civilizations elsewhere, grew rapidly, was creative and productive, and generated more wealth than any other place, making life better for everyone. It released all of the forces that make a strong country: creativity, competition, property rights, rule of law, and incentive to work. And, to the extent our freedom is reduced, all of the forces it releases are reduced, and our ability to create wealth and generate progress and an improved standard of living for everyone is also reduced.

Method. The second principle of America is method—how we make decisions. Our method is enshrined in the Constitution. While people will vehemently argue over particular decisions, they can more easily agree on how decisions should be made. Nobel Laureate F. A. Hayek said, "while agreement is not possible on most of the particular ends which will not be known except to those who pursue them…agreement on means can to a great extent be achieved precisely because it is not known which particular ends they will serve."[20] This facet of our nature gives us unity of purpose and allows us to rise above our disagreements on the proper resolution of political issues. Campaign Constitution was formed to improve the methods of decision making needed to restore our freedoms so that our country will be able to generate the wealth needed to meet the expectations of a changing population. An understanding of method entails an understanding of decision making—a concept little understood and much ignored in the formulation of national policy.

Human Nature. The third principle of America is human nature, which, next to the weather, has more influence on how we live than anything else. We learn much about human nature by studying the forces of history that have pushed us to where we are today. Knowledge of history gives us the knowledge of human nature, which is essential to making better predictions in the formulation of public policy.

Discipline. The fourth principle of America is discipline. A properly crafted democracy or republic has been shown to be the best discipline for controlling the passions of greed and power, which, if unchecked, undermine our freedoms. Discipline includes rule of law, religion, morality, reverence, and harmony and is essential to the preservation of freedom. Discipline is the essence of responsibility.

Action. The last principle of America is action. Unless we act to manage the relationships among us according to the principles that have bound us together and permitted us to have the freedom and resulting wealth for which America stands, our founding principles fall victim to entropy and will be crowded out by the efficiencies of tyranny.

The following comments, often attributed to the great German polymath von Goethe (1749–1832) but are actually those of William Hutchison Murray, bear reflection:

The moment one definitely commits oneself, then Providence moves too. All sorts of things occur to help one that would never otherwise have occurred. A whole stream of events issues from the decision raising in one's favor all manner of unforeseen incidents and meetings and material assistance which no man could have dreamt would come his way. Whatever you can do or dream you can do, begin it. Boldness has genius, power and magic in it. Begin it now.[21]

53

Essay 5:
Freedom

Commentaries on freedom are everywhere. In fact, there are no new ideas on the subject. People just express this important thought in different terms. Occasionally, a few of these terms catch on, only to get lost in time as other terms come into vogue. But it never hurts to repeat the thoughts of others on the subject.

For us, freedom is the right to choose responsibly. It is a right because, unless it is enforced and protected by government, it can be taken away by superior force. Responsibility is required because we know that this right must be exercised in a manner that does not unreasonably interfere with the rights of others. The right involves choice because we can choose not to do something or to do any of those infinite other opportunities perceived by us as free people. Although liberty is more unrestrained than freedom in a philosophical sense, we believe the Founding Fathers considered the two as largely the same. Our freedom is constrained not just by law but by our own conscience and sense of right and wrong and by social customs.

Freedom is like property because its essence, in the case of free-dom, is the individual's control over himself and, in the case of property, over things he controls to the exclusion of others. However, we have found with both freedom and property that the government steps in to regulate our choices whenever it decides that this is necessary in the public interest. Campaign Constitution was formed to check the federal government's supervision over our freedom and property and to transfer some of it to the States and to the people. There follow the views of a few others on the subject of freedom.

F. A. Hayek said in *Constitution of Liberty* (1960):

Though freedom is not a state of nature but an artifact of civilization, it did not arise from design. The institutions of freedom, like everything freedom has created, were not established because people foresaw the benefits they would bring. But, once its advantages were recognized, men began to perfect and extend the reign of freedom and, for that purpose, to inquire how a free society worked. This development of a theory of liberty took place mainly in the 18th century.

* * *

It is indeed a truth, which all the great apostles of freedom outside the rationalistic school have never tired of emphasizing, that freedom has never worked without deeply ingrained moral beliefs and that coercion can be reduced to a minimum only where individuals can be expected as a rule to conform voluntarily to certain principles.

* * *

There is as much need of moral rules in political as in individual action, and the consequences of successive collective decisions as well as those of individual decisions will be beneficial only if they are all in conformity with common principles.

Such moral rules for collective action are developed only with difficulty and very slowly. But this should be taken as an indication of their preciousness. The most important among the few principles of this kind that we have developed is individual freedom, which is most appropriate to regard as a moral principle of political action. Like all moral principles, it demands that it be accepted as a value in itself, as a principle that must be respected without our asking whether the consequences in the particular instance will be beneficial.[22]

F. A. Hayek said in *The Fatal Conceit* (1988):

…Hume may have been the first clearly to perceive that general freedom becomes possible by the natural moral instincts being "checked and restrained by subsequent judgment" according to "*justice*, or a regard to the property of others, *fidelity*, or the observance of promises [which have] become obligatory and acquire[d] an authority over mankind."[23]

Paul Woodruff, *First Democracy* (2005), discusses freedom (*eleutheria* in Greek) and says the Greeks learned the meaning of freedom by understanding the tyranny they did not want. He says:

Freedom needs an opposite. Before they knew what tyranny was, the Greeks had no notion of political freedom. Freedom from slavery is not the same thing, as we shall see. Generally, freedom has positive and negative sides. On the positive side, if you are free, then you are free to do something; the Athenians wanted to be free to take part in their own government. On the negative side, if you are free, there are certain things you are free from. In Athens, what the people wanted to be free from, more than anything else, was tyranny.…

The essence of their freedom was the right of any citizen to speak in the Assembly (*parrhesia*).[24]

Woodruff put great stock in the poets of the classical age because of their ability to express the emotions of the people. He notes that, when the Persian king asked the people of Samos for tribute, they asked Aesop for advice, and he replied:

Chance shows us two roads in life: one is the road of freedom, which has a rough beginning that is hard to walk, but an ending that is smooth and even; the other is the road of servitude, which has a level beginning, but an ending that is hard and dangerous.[25]

Woodruff quotes Solon in his comments on the tyrant Pisistratus:

Each of you follows the footprints of this fox,
And you all have empty minds,
For you watch only the tongue of the man, his slippery speech,
But you never look at what he actually does.[26]

In *Forever Flowing* (1970) the Russian novelist Vasily Grossman said:

I used to think freedom was freedom of speech, freedom of the press, freedom of conscience, but freedom is the whole life of everyone. Here is what it amounts to: You have to have the right to sow what you wish to, to make shoes or coats, to bake into bread the flour ground from the grain you have sown, and to sell it or not sell it as you wish: for the lathe operator, the steel worker, and the artist, it's a matter of being able to live as you wish and work as you wish and not as they order you to.

And it was with tragic clarity that the sacred law of all life defined itself: freedom of the individual human being is higher than anything else, and there is no goal, no purpose in the world, for which it may be sacrificed.[27]

John Cogswell, my father, said in the *Voice of the Plains* (1987):

Freedom is a dear, dear thing, and no responsible American wants to be part of denying freedom.... But freedom doesn't fall from heaven like rain. It has always had to be earned. Do you think our country would enjoy individual freedom if we were not full of millions of people who can read, study, and evaluate the events of the day?[28]

54

ESSAY 6:
HUMAN NATURE

M an cannot change his nature or the weather. Since the former is predictable, unlike the latter, man can craft his institutions by adding discipline in a way to protect himself from the weaknesses of his nature. This weakness is reflected in every life and documented by history. It is characterized by its preference for the insatiable intoxications of body, money, and power over the satiable intoxications of knowledge and the spirit. The effect of human nature on government is detailed in *The Discourses* by Niccolo Machiavelli (circa 1517), *The Federalist Papers* written mostly by Alexander Hamilton and James Madison (1787–88), *Democracy in America* by Alexis de Tocqueville (1835, 1840), *Liberalism* by Ludwig von Mises (1928), and the *Constitution of Liberty* by F. A. Hayek (1960). Yet, the subject is summarized most concisely by Professor Sidney Hook, who, in *The Hero in History* (1945), said:

> So long as they are permitted to grumble, most people are gratefully relieved to find someone to do their chores, whether they are household chores or political chores. Politics is a messy business, and life is short. We put up with a

great many evils in order to avoid the trouble of abolishing them.

*   *   *

Yet it is an old story that when we refuse to upset our "normal life" by plunging into the maelstrom, and entrust power to others, we awake someday to find that those to whom we entrusted it are well on their way to destroying "the normal life" we feared to interrupt. This is not only an old story but an ever-recurrent one. It will repeat itself until it is widely realized that political decisions must be made in any event; that responsibilities cannot be avoided by inaction or escape, for these have consequences; and that, considered even in its lowest terms, political effort and its attendant risks and troubles are a form of social insurance.[29]

We observe in human nature today a sentiment that rejects the past, not with a defined future but with an attitude that rights are greater than responsibilities. This sentiment is undisciplined by any morality, a submission to some regulating principle, or consciousness of service or obligation. This sentiment is vulnerable to leaders with charisma and demagoguery because without education it is uninformed. It assigns undeserved trust to the media, which is itself as weak and vulnerable as any individual person.

Professor Paul Woodruff provides a clear analysis of the meaning of human nature. He shows that there is a line between nature and custom that is not always easy to define. When we are born, we have a common nature, a need to survive and an ability to flourish (reason) within the customs established in the place of our birth. Since customs vary, they are not part of human nature. Further, what is part of human nature are the ramifications of our common potential, i.e., the ability to learn languages, to communicate, to live in communities, to participate in politics, and to contribute to citizen wisdom. In *First Democracy*, Woodruff says:

> Any government is government by ignorance. No one knows what the future will bring; no one knows whether a war we might wage will make us safer or put us more in danger. No one knows, but, luckily, knowledge is not everything. Even without knowledge we can use methods of decision making that are likely to lead to a good result. The ability to make good decisions without knowledge was called "*euboulia*" by the ancient Greeks—good judgment.
>
> Good judgment is what we need when we don't have knowledge. Good judgment involves many things. Of these the most important are being able to evaluate shaky arguments when shaky arguments are all we have, being open to adversary debate, and being willing to heed the wisdom of ordinary people.
>
> Citizen wisdom is what we exercise, as ordinary educated citizens, when we judge a contest of experts. It is not the same as "folk wisdom." Folk wisdom has many virtues, and it is the root of citizen wisdom. But it needs to be seasoned by education if it is to be open to new ideas. Citizen wisdom is capable of learning from experts, when it recognizes them. Citizen wisdom is what the citizens in a well-run democracy ought to have. It builds on common human abilities to perceive, reason, and judge, but it requires also healthy traditions and good education for all.[30]

In other words, Woodruff says, human nature must not be so thin as to accommodate only a goal of survival nor so thick as to include values proposed by others. Rather, it has to be thick enough to include values that flow from citizen wisdom but not so thick as to include values proposed by experts.

A good system of government reminds us of the importance of what there is about human nature that is greater than the goal of survival. The goal of survival is the basis of many pernicious values, including greed, dishonesty, and many of those acts forbidden by the Ten Commandments. Professor Woodruff says democracy properly understood "takes human imperfections into account better than any other ideal of government."[31] He adds, "Democracy was born out of a reverent awareness of human folly, and it was designed to prevent its leaders from having the unchecked power that could lead even the wisest of them from arrogance to foolishness."[32]

The aspect of human nature that lifts us out of the survival layer is documented by history. The history of formal thought, consciously or not, describes the human condition with recognition that there is something in it not of this world. We can define "not of this world" in many ways, but at its core there is a piece of divinity in all of us expressing itself as morality, religion, philosophy, natural law, or some other vital force of undefined inevitability. Yet, by any definition, life is shrouded with uncertainties, and efforts to undo them and provide certainties can have no effect other than to doom the human spirit.

Imbued with a nature so influenced, no amount of physical beauty or fitness, no amount of wealth or influence can bring a lasting smile. One can never get enough of these. Rather, concentration on what is unknown or what reminds us of what is unknown generates the intrigue that gives life meaning and happiness. Have you not noticed that those who study and search for knowledge or lose themselves in music bear a smile?

In the context of managing our daily lives with each other, a process we call government, there are those who define the uncertainties of life as freedom and others who define them in terms of risks to be avoided. Both definitions are grounded in a duality that pits an individual against the challenges of a universe of awe. And, in the competition between the two, the spirit of man, continuously recharged by an uncertain divinity, will always prevail and run parallel to those noble but failing efforts to satiate the individual with an unsatisfying largesse, which in the end is outdone by pain and misery.

chapter 55

Essay 7:
Rule of Law

Rule of law refers to the notion that everyone is subordinate to the law and no person is above the law. For this to occur, our laws must invite the respect of the people generally. Viktor Frankl said in his classic *Man's Search for Meaning* (1959) that there is nothing worse than the sense of injustice.[33] To avoid this, we have a system of laws, procedures, and decision making that ensures no one shall be denied life, liberty, or property for any reason except according to clearly written rules or standards that are predictable in their application and that provide a citizen a reasonable expectation as to the consequences of his action under the law. As such, the rule of law acts as a limitation on the power of government officials. Excessive government regulations and discretion have invited disrespect for the law, fostered the notion of rule of man, not rule of law, have increased the cost of using property, and delayed its application for beneficial uses. Courts are participants in this growing disrespect for law by their refusal to deal fairly with genuine controversies in favor of expediting resolution at the expense of achieving a just result and by their inability to deal rationally with the plethora of rules imposed by the government on commercial and personal activities.

56

ESSAY 8:
DECISION MAKING

Every decision involves a prediction. Many predictions have very little risk. For example, when you reach for a doorknob, you predict it will be where you see it. However, other predictions are less certain, and this is particularly so of those made by the government. Government policies are based on predictions about what will or will not happen if proposed policies are or are not adopted. When policies are adopted by the federal government based on predictions that turn out to be in error, the damage is great. When policies are adopted by a small town and turn out to be wrong, only the citizens of that town suffer.

Because of the foregoing observation, many have argued over the years that government closer to home is better. Thomas Jefferson made his case for this principle based on his discernment of human nature. Others have relied on other bases. Pope John XXIII in *Mater et Magistra* (1961)[34] made subsidiarity a moral principle. F. A. Hayek in his study of economics and political science reinforced the principle by his conclusion that, in making predictions, there will always be more that we do not know than we do know, with the effect that there always exists a high probability that a prediction in economics and political science will be incorrect.[35] More recently, behavioral psychologist Philip Tetlock, Ph.D., has concluded that the predictions of pundits, particularly in economics and political science, are more likely to be wrong than random chance.[36]

Since predictions are based on conclusions derived from facts applied to the values of a decision maker, his values become important to the average citizen. Although a statement of all facts relevant to any particular issue can never be entirely set forth, a conscientious person does the best he can, ever mindful of the admonition of Hayek that there are many facts likely to be left out, resulting in unintended consequences. Because of this, every decision involves commitment, risk, and courage. Citizens prefer people with values like theirs because they think their predictions will be more reliable. This preference is reinforced by the Greek notion that reasoning without knowledge, tested by adversary debate to reach what is most reasonable, may be a superior method of making a decision than an untested idea of the President, for example, that appeals to the credibility of the voters.

The person making a decision has values, and it is sometimes a competition in values that generates the competition in elections. Each opposing political candidate may have different views on public policy derived from different predictions based on different facts and understandings and experience. If they were equally informed with similar values, they would likely be closer together than most people think. Because of this, the education and dedication of public leaders become important qualifications for elective office. For example, every day we hear some television commentator or pundit talk about taxing the big corporations to raise revenue for the government as though they are bad and that everyone will agree to tax what they do not have. This statement illustrates that the proponent did not read Peter Drucker's book *Pension Fund Socialism* (1976),[37] which established at that time that the largest corporations in America are largely owned by the pension funds whose beneficiaries are the workers themselves, with the effect that higher taxes on big corporation result in higher taxes on the common man.

We also live in a world where television has become the sole source of news for many people, with fewer and fewer people reading newspapers or other intellectual commentaries. The term "media bias" surfaces because those who are more informed are frustrated that those less informed are speaking to millions of Americans and disseminating incorrect information.

The common reference to polling has degenerated our republic into a more democratic form of government, where short-term interests dominate long-term interests. Pure democracies become tyrannical, as noted by de Tocqueville and others. As far back as Cicero, active discussions were undertaken as to the proper form of government. It was because of these discussions that our Founding Fathers decided upon a republic and not a democracy. Having faith that they were right in this assessment, it is our duty to reinvigorate the pillars of a republic and endow our elected leaders with the statesmanship needed to govern our country in a changing world.

57

ESSAY 9:
FORCES OF HISTORY

At the primal level, life is about competition and selection. This truism in the world of commerce makes some men rich and others poor. This is not by chance. Some people are more able than others. They seize opportunities others do not see, and they marry and associate to reinforce their advantages. They are almost always a small segment of the total population. Yet, the people in this segment move in and out of it, depending on the quality of decisions they make. This segment invites envy, but the competition it instills benefits everyone.

The result of this competition is inequality. The poor man wants equality. The successful man wants freedom because it gave him what he has. He is sometimes called a conservative because he wants to preserve what he has. He is sometimes called a conservative because he wants to conserve freedom in order to give all persons, rich or poor, an opportunity to compete and seize available opportunities. By this definition, both the rich and the poor can be conservatives.

Yet, there are people who need more than they have and are unable to help themselves. We all want to help them, and there are many ways to do this. There are many reasons one could be in this group, but one thing is clear: As the size of this group grows, it becomes a strong political class supporting politicians who promise more and more help. When government promises become the best hope for a better life, the character of these persons diminishes, and the futility of caring for themselves increases.

Men, whether rich or poor, do share a common nature. They want the same things but possess different skills, use them differently, and see opportunities differently. As a group, they also share a common morality reinforced in most cases by religion and a reverence for a larger order of things over which they have no control. Our elected leaders fail Americans to the extent they ignore these commonalities in favor of appealing to a particular group to increase their potential power at the expense of our freedoms.

However, neither human nature, morality, religion, nor reverence can subdue a poor man's impulse for a better life. Thus begins the perennial cycle of all civilizations, which is continuing selection and revision of methods of government to level the playing field without subduing the freedom that produces the wealth needed by all of us and without creating an environment of despair that militates against general happiness.

These methods result in different kinds of government, each having conflicting factions. Political parties arise, each representing a base supporting a different method, sometimes radically and sometimes by degree. Further, these political parties are largely ignorant of the obstacles described, which are fated in all civilizations. Those in favor of leveling the playing field to generate equality falsely assume that the productive engines of a free people will continue unabated. Those in favor of freedom falsely assume that the poor will not get so large as to rebel successfully.

The Founding Fathers selected a republican form of government—a compromise between a democracy and an oligarchy. It has endured but has reached a precipice because efforts to appease the poor have overreached our ability to produce the wealth required.

Globalization has denied Congress the ability to influence the eco-nomic force of our country. Education has been unable to catch up with the growing complexity of our economy. Will and Ariel Durant, in *The Lessons of History* (1968), had this to say:

> It was such men who made Jefferson president—Jefferson who was as skeptical as Voltaire and as revolutionary as Rousseau. A government that governed least was admirably suited to liberate those individualistic energies that trans-formed America from a wilderness to a material Utopia, and from the child and ward to the rival and guardian of West-ern Europe. And while rural isolation enhanced the free-dom of the individual, national isolation provided liberty and security within protective seas. These and a hundred other conditions gave to America a democracy more basic and universal than history had ever seen.
>
> Many of these formative conditions have disappeared. Per-sonal isolation is gone through the growth of cities. Per-sonal independence is gone through the dependence of the worker upon tools and capital that he does not own, and upon conditions that he cannot control. War becomes more consuming, and the individual is helpless to understand its causes or to escape its effects. Free land is gone, though home ownership spreads—with a minimum of land. The once self-employed shopkeeper is in the toils of the big dis-tributor, and may echo Marx's complaint that everything is in chains. Economic freedom, even in the middle classes, becomes more and more exceptional, making political free-dom a consolatory pretense. And all this has come about not (as we thought in our hot youth) through the perversity of the rich, but through the impersonal fatality of economic development, and through the nature of man. Every advance

in the complexity of the economy puts an added premium upon superior ability, and intensifies the concentration of wealth, responsibility, and political power.[38]

As a result of the forces of history, our poor are increasing, the quality of education is declining, and the passions of our leaders proceed without reason or compromise or attention to history.

The intensity of the rhetoric has awakened the masses of Americans who care more about their country than they do about themselves. As Sidney Hook, *The Hero in History*, (1945), put it:

So long as they are permitted to grumble, most people are gratefully relieved to find someone to do their chores, whether they are household chores or political chores. Politics is a messy business, and life is short. We put up with a great many evils in order to avoid the trouble of abolishing them.

*   *   *

Yet it is an old story that when we refuse to upset our "normal life" by plunging into the maelstrom, and entrust power to others, we awake someday to find that those to whom we entrusted it are well on their way to destroying "the normal life" we feared to interrupt. This is not only an old story but an ever-recurrent one. It will repeat itself until it is widely realized that political decisions must be made in any event; that responsibilities cannot be avoided by inaction or escape, for these have consequences; and that, considered even in its lowest terms, political effort and its attendant risks and troubles are a form of social insurance.[39]

Concerned citizens will readily and rightly observe that our political leaders are largely chosen (elected) by chance, for it is a rare day that there are many votes separating one candidate from another at election time. They will observe that candidates say one thing and then do another when elected. They will observe corruption in office and the abuse of power. They will observe that candidates will make any promise to get elected. They will observe that many elected persons leave office with substantially more money than they had when elected. They will observe that too many voters assign credibility to political promises if they are corroborated by an uninformed media staffed by people just like them and easily as biased as anyone else. They will observe a stubborn reluctance to compromise, an unwillingness to put the country first when that is required, a bulk of arrogance, and a lack of statesmanship, reverence, and harmony.

If they read Cicero's *On the Republic*, they will read comments on which among democracy, oligarchy, or monarchy is the best form of government. They will learn that a free people intend to entrust their fortunes to the best men because of their wisdom and superiority of virtue and spirit. The problem is that the best men are soon seen as the:

> ...rich, prosperous, or born of famous families. For when, on account of this mistaken notion of the common people, the State begins to be ruled by the riches, instead of the virtue, of a few men, these rulers tenaciously retain the title, though they do not possess the character, of the "best"....
>
> But what can be nobler than the government of the State by virtue? For then the man who rules others is not himself a slave to any passion, but has already acquired for himself all those qualities.... Such a man imposes no law upon the people that he does not obey himself but puts his own life before his fellow-citizens as their law.[40]*
>
> Cicero, *The Republic* (Loeb's Classical Library ed., 2006).

---

*Cicero was trying to save the Roman Republic, but he lost. He was murdered on December 7, 43 B.C. His tongue was cut off and nailed to a post in the Roman forum. A few years thereafter, the Republic ended and the Empire began.

If they read further, they will find the following words of Cicero as inspiration to do something about the unhealthy balance that our Constitution in actual operation has bestowed upon us in this changing world:

> Thus, before our own time, the customs of our ancestors produced excellent men, and imminent men preserved our ancient customs and the institutions of their forefathers. But though the republic, when it came to us, was like a beautiful painting, whose colours, however, were already fading with age, our own time not only has neglected to freshen it by renewing the original colours, but has not even taken the trouble to preserve its configuration and, so to speak, its general outlines.... They have been, as we see, so completely buried in oblivion that they are not only no longer practiced, but already unknown. And what shall I say of the men? For the loss of our customs is due to the lack of men.... For it is through our own faults, not by any accident, that we retain only the form of the commonwealth, but have long since lost its substance....[41]

They may also read further and remark with interest the comments of Alexander Hamilton in *Federalist No. 33*:

> If the federal government should overpass the just bounds of its authority and make a tyrannical use of its powers, the people, whose creature it is, must appeal to the standard they have formed, and take such measures to redress the injury done to the Constitution as the exigency may suggest and prudence justify.[42]

These concerned citizens will rightly ask, "What is wrong with our country?" and "What can we do about it?" To the first question, their study will cause them to conclude that most of our leaders are without virtue, that they are embedded in money and power and have lost that passion to do the right thing. Sharon Krause, in *Liberalism With Honor* (2002), said:

> Contemporary liberalism [referring to democratic liberalism and not the philosophy of a liberal] needs a richer treatment of the motivations that drive political action. The current categories of self-interest and obligations to others are too limited to capture the full complexity of political agency. Honor offers an account of motivations that bridges the gap between self-interest and self-sacrifice, and that has both natural and historical connections to the defense of individual liberties.... A strong sense of agency is crucial to liberal government, and as long as political power is of an encroaching nature liberalism will have need of honor. Until the day when democracy is no longer vulnerable to overreaching majorities and the abuse of power, Americans occasionally will rely on the honor of the few who stand up to resist encroaching power, men and women willing to risk their necks to defend their liberties.[43]

Paul Woodruff in *Reverence, Renewing a Forgotten Virtue* (2001) said:

> Leadership (as opposed to tyranny) happens only where there is virtue, and reverence is the virtue on which leadership most depends....
>
> Reverence is the mainstay of a leader's good judgment. Good judgment is the intellectual virtue that guides deliberation in the absence of the relevant knowledge. Leaders in real life must make decisions without knowing for certain how those decisions will turn out.[44]

To the second question—"What can we do about it?"—our concerned citizens may find an answer from Niccolo Machiavelli, who wrote in *The Discourses* of necessity:

> After seeing that they would have to perish or cut their way out with the sword, Messius ordered his soldiers with the following words: "Follow me! You have no walls nor ditches to encounter, but only men armed like yourselves. Equals in valor, you have the advantage of necessity, the last and most powerful of weapons!"[45]

Another question is whether Campaign Constitution has a reasonable chance of changing the character of our leaders to inspire a change in the character of our nation. You have to be the judge of that. If you are willing to take the chance that Campaign Constitution can be successful, we solicit whatever support you can provide.

58

ESSAY 10: TYRANNY OF THE MAJORITY AND UNACCOUNTABLE MINORITIES

O ur voting patterns are in most cases very close to fifty-fifty. The percentage of voter turnout compared to the voting age population in presidential elections during the period from 1968 to 2008 has ranged from a high of 60.8 percent in 1968 to a low of 49.1 percent in 1996. Apart from these two numbers and discounting the effect of the electoral college, the percentage has ranged between 50.1 and 56.8. These elections have been won or lost by the votes of not more than 5 percent of the voters and sometimes by substantially less. What does this mean for those who do not vote or are too young to vote?

The party that wins claims sanction to impose its views on the whole despite being in office because of only a small margin of approximately half of the voting age population. The losing party makes countervailing claims, but, since it is not accountable, makes them more appealing to obtain popular support in the next election. This dynamic polarizes the political parties and their leaders because potential power is valued more than the best interests of our country.

Statesmen trying to do the right thing do not have a chance. They become stereotyped and predictable and are shunted to the side, leaving power brokers with their capacity for compromise to have a larger share of power. This problem can be remedied by requiring a super-majority vote, which means that disagreeing factions must come together to get anything done.

In many cases, minorities end up ruling the country. They have great passion, attend meetings, write letters to the editor, and have ways of taking advantage of the apathy of the majority. It is time for all of us to be alert and take an interest in the consequences of poorly managed government and balance the tyranny of the majority with unaccountability of the minority.

59

ESSAY 11:
WEALTH

The "haves" and the "have nots"—the tension between these classes has endured as long as society itself. We are naturally fearful of inequality in the distribution of wealth, human capital, and political influence. The reason is these operate as power factors, which can deprive us of our freedom. The ancient Greeks were afraid of the rich and protected themselves by using a lottery and developing democratic institutions to diminish their power.

Politicians today appeal to the "have nots" by demagogic pandering. In doing so, they unwittingly preach for the elimination of our democracy. The redistribution of wealth always defeats the wealth-creating machine and lays the foundation for tyranny. Experience tells us that taking from the rich and giving to the poor will never work because, when we change the system to do this, the system that generated the wealth in the first place disappears. Ludwig von Mises said:

What is most criticized in our social order is the inequality in the distribution of wealth and income. There are rich and poor; there are very rich and very poor. The way out is not far to seek: the equal distribution of all wealth.

The first objection to this proposal is that it will not help the situation much because those of moderate means far outnumber the rich, so that each individual could expect from such a distribution only a quite insignificant increment in his standard of living. This is certainly correct, but the argument is not complete. Those who advocate equality of income distribution *overlook the most important point*, namely, that the total available for distribution, the annual product of social labor, is not independent of the manner in which it is divided. The fact that that product today is as great as it is, is not a natural or technological phenomenon independent of all social conditions, but entirely the result of our social institutions. Only because inequality of wealth is possible in our social order, only because it stimulates everyone to produce as much as he can and at the lowest cost, does mankind today have at its disposal the total annual wealth now available for consumption. Were this incentive to be destroyed, productivity would be so greatly reduced that the portion that an equal distribution would allot to each individual would be far less than what even the poorest receives today.

The inequality of income distribution has, however, still a second function quite as important as the one already mentioned: it makes possible the luxury of the rich.

Many foolish things have been said and written about luxury. Against luxury consumption it has been objected that it is unjust that some should enjoy great abundance while others are in want. This argument seems to have some merit.

But it only seems so. For if it can be shown that luxury consumption performs a useful function in the system of social cooperation, then the argument will be proved invalid. This, however, is what we shall seek to demonstrate.

To form a correct conception of the social significance of luxury consumption, one must first of all realize that the concept of luxury is an altogether relative one. Luxury consists in a way of living that stands in sharp contrast to that of the great mass of one's contemporaries. The conception of luxury is, therefore, essentially historical. Many things that seem to us necessities today were once considered as luxuries.... The luxury of today is the necessity of tomorrow. Every advance first comes into being as the luxury of a few rich people, only to become, after a time, the indispensable necessity taken for granted by everyone. Luxury consumption provides industry with the stimulus to discover and introduce new things. It is one of the dynamic factors in our economy. To it we owe the progressive innovations by which the standard of living of all strata of the population has been gradually raised.

Most of us have no sympathy with the rich idler who spends his life in pleasure without ever doing any work. But even he fulfills a function in the life of the social organism. He sets an example of luxury that awakens in the multitude a consciousness of new needs and gives industry the incentive to fulfill them.[46]

Richard Epstein, professor of law, put it another way: "One of the fundamental mistakes of the egalitarians is they're so interested in trying to minimize differences that they don't understand the completely adverse effects that it has on the size of the pie."[47]

CURRENT DISTRIBUTION OF WEALTH AND INCOME

One can begin by asking what is the distribution of wealth and income in America. Professor G. William Domhoff, Sociology Department, University of California, published a paper on the subject. He shows that in 1983, the top 20 percent of households owned 81.3 percent of the wealth, leaving the bottom 80 percent owning 18.7 percent. By 2007, these numbers were 85.1 percent and 15 percent, respectively. Interestingly, the top 1 percent in 1983 had 33.8 percent of the wealth and by 2007 had 34.6 percent of the wealth. In other words, there has not been much change over the past thirty years.

From a more historical point of view, the top 1 percent had 36.7 percent of the wealth in 1922, which increased to 44.2 percent by 1929 and then decreased to 27.1 percent by 1949. The percentage inched up to 34.4 in 1965 and then hit a low in 1976 of 19.9, after which time it hit a high of 38.5 percent in 1995, only to decrease to 34.6 percent in 2007. These are just percentages, and, in all likelihood, the people within these percentages change every day.

In 2000, Switzerland's top 10 percent held 71.3 percent of the wealth, and the United States was second with 69.8 percent. Denmark, France, Sweden, the United Kingdom, and Canada were in the range of 53 to 65 percent, with Germany at 44.4 percent.

Economists have generated a Gini coefficient, which allows them to compare income inequality. A Gini coefficient of zero means everyone has the same income, and a Gini coefficient of one hundred means one person in the country has all the income. The United States is ninety-fifth out of 134 countries studied, meaning thirty-nine countries have more income inequality. Sweden has a Gini coefficient of 23, Canada of 32.1, the United Kingdom 34, Egypt 34.4, India 36.8, China 41.5, Russia 42.3, and the United States 45.

Interestingly, Professor Domhoff concluded that higher income taxes are not particularly progressive, that the more wealth one has, the more power he has, and that transfer payments are slightly more effective than taxes in generating more equality of income, but neither one has a material effect. For example, IRS records show that there are 235,000 taxpayers who earn over $1 million per year and who collectively earn $726 billion per year. Assuming they pay 15 percent of this in taxes, there remains $617 billion to be taxed. If all of this were taxed, it would cover the federal government's $4 billion daily deficit for 154 days, a little over five months. Can we suppose these 235,000 people would work as hard the next year as they did the year they made $726 billion and paid all of it to Uncle Sam? What does it tell us when our allegedly responsible leaders want to raise taxes on the rich? This can have no rational appeal but certainly foments the visceral envy the poor have for the rich, the same envy Moses warned us about 3,500 years ago.

DOES INEQUALITY IN WEALTH AND INCOME AFFECT THE QUALITY OF AMERICA?

Unanswered by Professor Domhoff is the more important question, which is whether more equality in wealth and income will make a better America. For an answer to this question, one can read numerous economic abstracts, which circle the problem but generate no particular answers. We suppose there is a balance that ensures the preservation of harmony and that also diminishes the collective fear of centralized power in the few and increases the incentives to work and to create wealth and better our lives and others. However, in a changing world, this balance likely changes every day in one direction or another.

From a longer term point of view, one can observe from the economic abstracts that in the mid-1950s America's success was attributed to the accumulation of capital. Later, economists wondered whether the capital was accumulated because of inherited English institutions and Protestant beliefs. Others wondered, since the Pilgrims and their progeny were largely equal, each having to work to survive, whether the general equality among them in wealth and income provided the stimulus that generated American growth. This equality, for example, tended to influence more democratic political institutions, more investment in public goods and infrastructure, and institutions that offered relatively broad access to economic opportunity. Other economists have attributed America's success to its distribution of lands, patent laws, its broad voting laws, and its public education and private banking, which combined to lower thresholds for access to economic opportunities. Other economists have suggested that the availability of commodities predicts the middle class share of income, which in turn predicts development and therefore confirms that high inequality becomes a barrier to development. Other economists are looking at the long-term effects that historic events can have on current economic development and have concluded that history really does matter since it reflects all of the cultural, geographical, and weather conditions as of a period of time.

In a copyrighted paper published by the National Bureau of Economic Research, *Misperceptions About the Magnitude and Timing of Changes in American Income Inequality*, (Robert J. Gordon, 2009), Professor Gordon, Department of Economics, Northwestern University, concluded that not only had the increase of inequality been exaggerated, but it reversed itself after 2000. He stated:

> The rise of American inequality has been exaggerated in magnitude, and its impact is now largely in the past. Standard commentary laments the slow growth of median real household income and concludes that over the past three decades (1979–2007) the gap between growth of income and productivity has been 1.46 percent per year. But this "conventional" gap measure is riddled with measurement and conceptual inconsistencies. Our "alternative" gap measure grows at only 0.16 percent over the same period, only one-tenth as rapidly as the conventional gap, and it does not

grow at all during the 1979–1995 period when inequality was growing fastest. In fact, we show that income-productivity gaps have virtually nothing to do with inequality. The alternative growth gap is zero when inequality grew fastest before 1995, became negative when inequality grew further during 1995–2000, and was strongly positive in 2000–2007 when inequality decreased.[48]

The most that can be said is that nobody knows what the magic formula is, which means we have a duty to set the available facts before the people and let the voting booth decide what is best for America in terms of issues associated with inequality of wealth and income. So far as we are concerned, as long as the ownership of wealth remains in an envelope of historic changes, there is not likely much to worry about. Although it is acknowledged that the few have more power than the many by reason of this wealth, they have less power in the voting booth and must behave responsibly and make convincing cases to keep their wealth. This provides incentive to marshal it and invest it wisely.

WHAT ABOUT THE REPEAL OF THE ESTATE TAX AND TAXING THE RICH?

Some argue for repeal of the estate tax. Others argue to keep it to raise revenue. The issue is whether the government upon receipt of the revenue spends it more wisely than private individuals.

Higher estate taxes, with a generous exemption to protect farmers and small businesses, which provide the bulk of employment in America, are not likely to persuade the wealthy to move to other countries if they pay any attention to the Gini coefficient discussed above. Moreover, one has to remember, as with income inequality, that the members of the group who have the most of both change over time and provide incentive to others to transit from lower stations to higher stations on the economic ladder. It might be helpful to condition the repeal of the estate tax on the elimination of the national debt, which would likely give the wealthy more incentive to seek better management of the government rather than more tax breaks. As for the case for repeal, we have seen no evidence that the wisdom of the generation that made the wealth can send the wisdom along with the wealth. Moreover, we believe a case can be made that the money created by increasing the national debt mostly ends up with the wealthy, so it makes some sense to earmark estate tax revenue to eliminate this debt.

The only reason to increase the taxes on the rich is the assumption that the rich are not efficiently utilizing the money they have for the benefit of everyone and that the government could do a better job. The assumption continues that the rich are either lazy or poor investors, neither of which comports with the facts. There will always be a cost in terms of economic efficiency in any redistribution or transfer scheme that has to be measured before any of those schemes are formally approved.

The shortage of available evidence that extant inequalities of wealth or income are hurting America suggests that rhetoric regarding the "haves" versus the "have nots" is demagogic in character for the purpose of obtaining political power and influence, which has the unintended consequence of diminishing the quality of our government and nation.

Noted philosopher and sociologist, James Q. Wilson, recently said: "It is easy to suppose that raising taxes on the rich would provide more money to help the poor. But the problem facing the poor is not too little money, but too few skills and opportunities to advance themselves."[49] He also noted that the Gini coefficient in Greece has been falling, thereby reducing income inequality. Yet, we all know what is going on in Greece.

THE MONOPOLY EFFECT

We all know if we play "Monopoly" long enough one person usually ends up with the money. This could be the game but also could be luck or the nature of things. Those who make lots of money are good at what they do and make available their products to the public for a good price. Yet, there is no evidence that what they are good at is passed on to their progeny. As a matter of policy, it is not a good idea to allow wealth to accumulate in a vessel of inferior aptitude, though clearly mismanagement by progeny will cause the wealth to dissipate into the hands of others. The common use of trusts and foundations and the relaxation of the rule against perpetuities are other factors that we defer to another day but that need watching.

Matt Ridley in *The Origins of Virtue* (1996) reminds us that "where authority replaces reciprocity, the sense of community fades"[50] and that growing statism has ruinous consequences. In brilliant prose, he explains how "trust is the foundation of virtue"[51] and implicit in all of the essential cultural attributes of human nature even before governments were established, including morality, money, contracts, welfare, and society. The irony is that, as the government grows, the essential elements of community and cooperation diminish. He says, "If we are to recover social harmony and virtue, if we are to build back into society the virtues that made it work for us, it is vital that we reduce the power and scope of the state."[52]

Ridley observed that the division of labor creates efficiency and wealth but also polarizes the people. Ortega y Gasset in *The Revolt of the Masses* (1932) observed that the specialization associated with division of labor has brought about a "rebirth of primitivism and barbarism."[53] The reason:

> By specializing him, civilization has made him hermetic and self-satisfied with his limitation; but this very inner feeling of dominance and worth will induce him to wish to predominate outside his specialty.[54]

Thus, this man, though knowledgeable in his own field, is ignorant of the historical conditions requisite for the continuation of the very civilization that made him knowledgeable in his field in the first place.

It is no wonder that man, having satiated himself, has turned to analyzing why his government is no longer acceptable, either because there is not enough freedom or because there is not enough bounty. The question is whether the ruinous consequences of excessive government power occur from excessive private power. Under present-day conditions, the answer seems to be "no."

CONCLUSION

There is no evidence that lowering the share of income and wealth held by the wealthy would improve the country. This share has gone up or down depending on the overall health of America and the world. The people in these percentages change all of the time. As long as the rich's share stays within historical envelopes, it would seem the division of wealth reflects human nature and the natural inequality in people. One thing is clear: The rich are better managers of the wealth they have than the government, and, as long as this is true, the resulting benefits accrue, directly or indirectly, to all Americans.

60

ESSAY 12:
CLASS WARFARE

Freedom and equality are everlasting enemies. When one rises, the other falls. Political parties are divided by this conflict. Some conservatives want to conserve the past to preserve what they have acquired. If they become entrenched, the wealthy indeed have more power, and there are more barriers for others to climb the economic ladder and upset the status quo. Other conservatives want to conserve freedom. If these conservatives have their way, the future is uncertain because its course cannot be predicted, but every man has a chance to pursue his own happiness and live in freedom. Liberals want to advance social justice, which can only occur by taking wealth from some and giving it to others based upon their confidence that government persons, academia, and experts can make decisions superior to those which a free people would make. If liberals become too aggressive with their goal, they destroy the wealth their views require and, most generally, fail to realize that their views diminish the very freedom that makes possible the production of the very wealth they wish to bestow upon the less fortunate.

Almost everyone wants to help those who cannot help themselves, with resulting debate centered on the method of doing so. Reliance on freedom is not politically rewarding because its benefits are not easily discernible, and freedom as the procuring cause is not obvious. Special programs are politically attractive because their benefits are more obvious, and those persons specially benefited attribute their benefits to those who advanced those benefits in Congress.

The great debate between John Maynard Keynes (1883–1946) and F. A. Hayek (1899–1992), which frames the current economic debate in America, illustrates the importance of method. Keynes, fully aware of the cyclical features of capitalism with high unemployment in the trough periods, advocated government planning and spending to maintain consumer demand, production, and employment. Hayek, on the other hand, argued that the unemployment problem was best left to corrections in the economy, which would naturally come about. He was concerned that there had to be limits to government planning or the country would trend toward socialism, fascism, tyranny, and the loss of freedom. Keynes was not unconcerned about the loss of freedom but argued that government planning and spending would not threaten it. He said:

> But the planning should take place in a community in which as many people as possible, both leaders and followers, wholly share your own moral position.... Moderate planning will be safe if those carrying it out are rightly oriented in their own minds and hearts to the moral issue. This is in fact already true of some of them. But the truth is that there is also an important section who could almost be said to want planning not in order to enjoy its fruits but because morally they hold ideas exactly the opposite of yours, and wish to serve not God but the devil.

* * *

Dangerous acts can be done safely in a community which thinks and feels rightly, which would be the way to hell if they were executed by those who think and feel wrongly.

* * *

There is no reason why, in a society which has reached the general level of wealth which ours has attained, [this] kind of security [laws alleviating poverty and ill health] should not be guaranteed to all without endangering general freedom.... Whether those who rely on the community should indefinitely enjoy all the same liberties as the rest...might well cause serious and perhaps even dangerous political problems.[55]

Keynes agreed with Cicero, who also believed government should rest on a moral foundation. The problem today is that the required moral foundation is crumbling. The so-called Judeo-Christian culture has been diminished according to some scholars. Secularism is on the rise. Persons of different faiths and cultures are growing. All of this creates special challenges to a system created by men who generally had common beliefs.

This crumbling effect is illustrated by the voting on the Affordable Care Act. In December 2009, it passed the House of Representative by a vote of 219 to 212, with no Republicans voting for it and thirty-four Democrats voting against it. It passed in the Senate by a vote of 60 to 40, exactly what was needed to avoid cloture. A Nebraska senator got the federal government to pay Nebraska's Medicaid bill in exchange for his vote. In January 2011, the House voted to repeal 245 to 189, with no Republicans voting against repeal. The Senate voted against repeal 51 to 47. The most one can observe from this is that voting is divided at a moral level when our leaders would seek to impose a systemic change on our country consuming

18 percent of GDP annually without having the general consensus of the people and their representatives.

Those in need of wealth will vote for liberals. Demography tells us they will soon be a majority, and then they will control the nature of our government and have the power to destroy the harmony so essential to a unified purpose. This will destabilize our government and likely cause inflation. Hayek tells us that social justice is an illusion, but an illusion can be strong enough to ruin a government. The preservation of a free country and a government that supports a free country is no easy challenge. It takes informed citizens and statesmen with discipline and vision. Once lost, history tells us that dictators are more likely to appear than not, and thereafter they are difficult to replace with a more suitable form of government. Greece lost its democracy in 322 B.C. and dreamt for its return, which did not occur until 1829, 2,151 years after it had been lost.

Hamilton forewarned us of this problem in *Federalist No. 1*, where he said:

> ...it will be equally forgotten that the vigor of government is essential to the security of liberty; that, in the contemplation of a sound and well-informed judgment, their interests can never be separated; and that a dangerous ambition more often lurks behind the specious mask of zeal for the rights of the people than under the forbidding appearance of zeal for the firmness and efficiency of government. History will teach us that the former has been found a much more certain road to the introduction of despotism than the latter, and that of those men who have overturned the liberties of republics, the greatest number have begun their career by paying an obsequious court to the people, commencing demagogues and ending tyrants.[56]

The harmony essential to good government is easier to maintain where there is commonality. In a nation glorifying diversity, our only chance for harmony is if all of us accord dignity to our differences. As Jonathan Sacks said in *The Dignity of Difference* (2002), "Conversation—respectful, engaged, reciprocal, calling forth some of our greatest powers of empathy and understanding—is the moral form of a world governed by the dignity of difference."[57] If morality is essential to good government, as argued by Keynes, Sachs has set forth the challenge before us.

The need for harmony between disagreeing parties has never been greater. Paul Woodruff was blunt: "Without harmony, there is no democracy."[58] This essential ingredient is no easy term to define because it depends on so many things—respect, reverence, integrity, courage, virtue, and morality, to name a few. One could sum up the meaning of harmony by saying a nation that has harmony has character. And character allows us to accept differences, even though we disagree with them. The loss of harmony is historically associated with civil war, moral collapse, and atrocity.

We have harmony when what holds us together is stronger than what pulls us apart. We saw the former after 9-11, but we have witnessed differences that reinforce the latter ever since the Iraq War. For most of our history, our harmony was illustrated by a plethora of common interests grounded in ideas, morality, and the Constitution. Yet, today we have managed our government in a way that divides the rich and the poor, which heralds the conflict in ancient Greece, which witnessed a conflict between the people (poor) and the oligarchs (the rich and the few). The singular advantage of the Greeks was that they had experience in dealing with the consequences of such conflicts and adjusted their constitution to deal with them. Both sides knew how awful life could be if they did not work together. George Washington understood this when he said in his Farewell Address (1796), "Harmony, liberal intercourse with all nations, are recommended by policy, humanity, and interest."[59] The Civil War further reinforced the need for harmony, and that was followed by the serious conflicts among the pioneers, farmers, ranchers, and American Indians, who eventually learned the same lesson.

We have seen the need for harmony during the many wars we have fought, but we seem to have lost the need for harmony in dealing with public policy issues affecting everyday Americans. Declining education, growing entitlements, voter apathy, and misinformation are factors that contribute to the loss of harmony. If our foundation were to be broad-sided by financial collapse, a distinct possibility considering the size of our national debt, we citizens need to be braced to work with each other to persevere through the tough times that history teaches us can be very unpleasant.

We believe reforms can be made to our Constitution that have a chance of restoring our country to the noble vision inspired by our Founding Fathers, even though the risks today are as great as they were then. They are just different risks. But, properly managed, an acceptable balance of the conflicting values of Americans is still possible.

THE DECLARATION OF INDEPENDENCE

Action of Second Continental Congress, July 4, 1776
The Unanimous Declaration of the Thirteen
United States of America

WHEN in the Course of human events, it becomes necessary for one people to dissolve the political bands which have connected them with another, and to assume among the powers of the earth, the separate and equal station to which the Laws of Nature and of Nature's God entitle them, a decent respect to the opinions of mankind requires that they should declare the causes which impel them to the separation.

WE hold these truths to be self-evident, that all men are created equal, that they are endowed by their Creator with certain unalienable Rights, that among these are Life, Liberty and the pursuit of Happiness.—That to secure these rights, Governments are instituted among Men, deriving their just powers from the consent of the governed,—That whenever any Form of Government becomes destructive of these ends, it is the Right of the People to alter or to abolish it, and to institute new Government, laying its foundation on such principles and organizing its powers in such form, as to them shall seem most likely to effect their Safety and Happiness. Prudence, indeed, will dictate that Governments long established should not be changed for light and transient causes; and accordingly all experience hath shewn, that mankind are more disposed to suffer, while evils are sufferable, than to right themselves by abolishing the forms to which they are accustomed. But when a long train of abuses and usurpations, pursuing invariably the same Object evinces a design to reduce them under absolute Despotism, it is their right, it is their duty, to throw off such Government, and to provide new Guards for their future security.—Such has been the patient sufferance of these Colonies; and such is now the necessity which constrains them to alter their former Systems of Government. The history of the present King of Great Britain is a history of repeated injuries and usurpations, all having in direct object the establishment of an absolute Tyranny over these States. To prove this, let Facts be submitted to a candid world.

HE has refused his Assent to Laws, the most wholesome and necessary for the public good.

HE has forbidden his Governors to pass Laws of immediate and pressing importance, unless suspended in their operation till his Assent should be obtained; and when so suspended, he has utterly neglected to attend to them.

HE has refused to pass other Laws for the accommodation of large districts of people, unless those people would relinquish the right of Representation in the Legislature, a right inestimable to them and formidable to tyrants only.

HE has called together legislative bodies at places unusual, uncomfortable, and distant from the depository of their public Records, for the sole purpose of fatiguing them into compliance with his measures.

HE has dissolved Representative Houses repeatedly, for opposing with manly firmness his invasions on the rights of the people.

HE has refused for a long time, after such dissolutions, to cause others to be elected; whereby the Legislative powers, incapable of Annihilation, have returned to the People at large for their exercise; the State remaining in the mean time exposed to all the dangers of invasion from without, and convulsions within.

HE has endeavoured to prevent the population of these States; for that purpose obstructing the Laws for Naturalization of Foreigners; refusing to pass others to encourage their migrations hither, and raising the conditions of new Appropriations of Lands.

HE has obstructed the Administration of Justice, by refusing his Assent to Laws for establishing Judiciary powers.

HE has made Judges dependent on his Will alone, for the tenure of their offices, and the amount and payment of their salaries.

HE has erected a multitude of New Offices, and sent hither swarms of Officers to harass our people, and eat out their substance.

HE has kept among us, in times of peace, Standing Armies without the Consent of our legislatures.

HE has affected to render the Military independent of and superior to the Civil power.

HE has combined with others to subject us to a jurisdiction foreign to our constitution, and unacknowledged by our laws; giving his Assent to their Acts of pretended Legislation:

FOR Quartering large bodies of armed troops among us:

FOR protecting them, by a mock Trial, from punishment for any Murders which they should commit on the Inhabitants of these States:

FOR cutting off our Trade with all parts of the world:

FOR imposing Taxes on us without our Consent:

FOR depriving us in many cases, of the benefits of Trial by Jury:

FOR transporting us beyond Seas to be tried for pretended offences:

FOR abolishing the free System of English Laws in a neighbouring Province, establishing therein an Arbitrary government, and enlarging its Boundaries so as to render it at once an example and fit instrument for introducing the same absolute rule into these Colonies:

FOR taking away our Charters, abolishing our most valuable Laws, and altering fundamentally the Forms of our Governments:

FOR suspending our own Legislatures, and declaring themselves invested with power to legislate for us in all cases whatsoever.

HE has abdicated Government here, by declaring us out of his Protection and waging War against us.

HE has plundered our seas, ravaged our Coasts, burnt our towns, and destroyed the lives of our people.

HE is at this time transporting large Armies of foreign Mercenaries to compleat the works of death, desolation and tyranny, already begun with circumstances of Cruelty & perfidy scarcely paralleled in the most barbarous ages, and totally unworthy of the Head of a civilized nation.

HE has constrained our fellow Citizens taken Captive on the high Seas to bear Arms against their Country, to become the executioners of their friends and Brethren, or to fall themselves by their Hands.

HE has excited domestic insurrections amongst us, and has endeavoured to bring on the inhabitants of our frontiers, the merciless Indian Savages, whose known rule of warfare, is an undistinguished destruction of all ages, sexes and conditions.

IN every stage of these Oppressions We have Petitioned for Redress in the most humble terms: Our repeated Petitions have been answered only by repeated injury. A Prince whose character is thus marked by every act which may define a Tyrant, is unfit to be the ruler of a free people.

NOR have We been wanting in attentions to our British brethren. We have warned them from time to time of attempts by their legislature to extend an unwarrantable jurisdiction over us. We have reminded them of the circumstances of our emigration and settlement here. We have appealed to their native justice and magnanimity, and we have conjured them by the ties of our common kindred to disavow these usurpations, which, would inevitably interrupt our connections and correspondence. They too have been deaf to the voice of justice and of consanguinity. We must, therefore, acquiesce in the necessity, which denounces our Separation, and hold them, as we hold the rest of mankind, Enemies in War, in Peace Friends.

We, therefore, the Representatives of the **united States of America,** in General Congress, Assembled, appealing to the Supreme Judge of the world for the rectitude of our intentions, do, in the Name, and by Authority of the good People of these Colonies, solemnly publish and declare, That these United Colonies are, and of Right ought to be **Free and Independent States;** that they are Absolved from all Allegiance to the British Crown, and that all political connection between them and the State of Great Britain, is and ought to be totally dissolved; and that as Free and Independent States, they have full Power to levy War, conclude Peace, contract Alliances, establish Commerce, and to do all other Acts and Things which Independent States may of right do. And for the support of this Declaration, with a firm reliance on the protection of divine Providence, we mutually pledge to each other our Lives, our Fortunes and our sacred Honor.

(The 56 signatures on the Declaration were arranged in six columns.)

Georgia:
Button Gwinnett
Lyman Hall
George Walton

North Carolina:
William Hooper
Joseph Hewes
John Penn

South Carolina:
Edward Rutledge
Thomas Heyward, Jr.
Thomas Lynch, Jr.
Arthur Middleton

Massachusetts:
John Hancock

Maryland:
Samuel Chase
William Paca
Thomas Stone
Charles Carroll of
    Carrollton

Virginia:
George Wythe
Richard Henry Lee
Thomas Jefferson
Benjamin Harrison
Thomas Nelson, Jr.
Francis Lightfoot Lee
Carter Braxton

Pennsylvania:
Robert Morris
Benjamin Rush
Benjamin Franklin
John Morton
George Clymer
James Smith
George Taylor
James Wilson
George Ross

Delaware:
Caesar Rodney
George Read
Thomas McKean

New York:
William Floyd
Philip Livingston
Francis Lewis
Lewis Morris

New Jersey:
Richard Stockton
John Witherspoon
Francis Hopkinson
John Hart
Abraham Clark

New Hampshire:
Josiah Bartlett
William Whipple

Massachusetts:
Samuel Adams
John Adams
Robert Treat Paine
Elbridge Gerry

Rhode Island:
Stephen Hopkins
William Ellery

Connecticut:
Roger Sherman
Samuel Huntington
William Williams
Oliver Wolcott

New Hampshire:
Matthew Thornton

B

CONSTITUTION OF THE UNITED STATES OF AMERICA[60]

(Reproduced from The Constitution Society)

We the People of the United States, in Order to form a more perfect Union, establish Justice, insure domestic Tranquility, provide for the common defence, promote the general Welfare, and secure the Blessings of Liberty to ourselves and our Posterity, do ordain and establish this Constitution for the United States of America.

ARTICLE. I.

Section. 1.[61] All legislative Powers herein granted shall be vested in a Congress of the United States, which shall consist of a Senate and House of Representatives.

Section. 2. The House of Representatives shall be composed of Members chosen every second Year by the People of the several States, and the Electors in each State shall have the Qualifications requisite for Electors of the most numerous Branch of the State Legislature.

No Person shall be a Representative who shall not have attained to the Age of twenty five Years, and been seven Years a Citizen of the

United States, and who shall not, when elected, be an Inhabitant of that State in which he shall be chosen.

Representatives and direct Taxes shall be apportioned among the several States which may be included within this Union, according to their respective Numbers, which shall be determined by adding to the whole Number of free Persons, including those bound to Service for a Term of Years, and excluding Indians not taxed, three fifths of all other Persons.[62] The actual Enumeration shall be made within three Years after the first Meeting of the Congress of the United States, and within every subsequent Term of ten Years, in such Manner as they shall by Law direct. The Number of Representatives shall not exceed one for every thirty Thousand, but each State shall have at Least one Representative; and until such enumeration shall be made, the State of New Hampshire shall be entitled to chuse three, Massachusetts eight, Rhode-Island and Providence Plantations one, Connecticut five, New-York six, New Jersey four, Pennsylvania eight, Delaware one, Maryland six, Virginia ten, North Carolina five, South Carolina five, and Georgia three.

When vacancies happen in the Representation from any State, the Executive Authority thereof shall issue Writs of Election to fill such Vacancies.

The House of Representatives shall chuse their Speaker and other Officers; and shall have the sole Power of Impeachment.

Section. 3. The Senate of the United States shall be composed of two Senators from each State, chosen by the Legislature thereof,[63] for six Years; and each Senator shall have one Vote.

Immediately after they shall be assembled in Consequence of the first Election, they shall be divided as equally as may be into three Classes. The Seats of the Senators of the first Class shall be vacated at the Expiration of the second Year, of the second Class at the Expiration of the fourth Year, and of the third Class at the Expiration of the sixth Year, so that one third may be chosen every second Year; and if

Vacancies happen by Resignation, or otherwise, during the Recess of the Legislature of any State, the Executive thereof may make temporary Appointments until the next Meeting of the Legislature, which shall then fill such Vacancies.[64]

No Person shall be a Senator who shall not have attained to the Age of thirty Years, and been nine Years a Citizen of the United States, and who shall not, when elected, be an Inhabitant of that State for which he shall be chosen.

The Vice President of the United States shall be President of the Senate, but shall have no Vote, unless they be equally divided.

The Senate shall chuse their other Officers, and also a President pro tempore, in the Absence of the Vice President, or when he shall exercise the Office of President of the United States.

The Senate shall have the sole Power to try all Impeachments. When sitting for that Purpose, they shall be on Oath or Affirmation. When the President of the United States is tried, the Chief Justice shall preside: And no Person shall be convicted without the Concurrence of two thirds of the Members present.

Judgment in Cases of Impeachment shall not extend further than to removal from Office, and disqualification to hold and enjoy any Office of honor, Trust or Profit under the United States: but the Party convicted shall nevertheless be liable and subject to Indictment, Trial, Judgment and Punishment, according to Law.

Section. 4. The Times, Places and Manner of holding Elections for Senators and Representatives, shall be prescribed in each State by the Legislature thereof; but the Congress may at any time by Law make or alter such Regulations, except as to the Places of chusing Senators.

The Congress shall assemble at least once in every Year, and such Meeting shall be on the first Monday in December,[65] unless they shall by Law appoint a different Day.

Section. 5. Each House shall be the Judge of the Elections, Returns and Qualifications of its own Members, and a Majority of each shall constitute a Quorum to do Business; but a smaller Number may adjourn from day to day, and may be authorized to compel the Attendance of absent Members, in such Manner, and under such Penalties as each House may provide.

Each House may determine the Rules of its Proceedings, punish its Members for disorderly Behaviour, and, with the Concurrence of two thirds, expel a Member.

Each House shall keep a Journal of its Proceedings, and from time to time publish the same, excepting such Parts as may in their Judgment require Secrecy; and the Yeas and Nays of the Members of either House on any question shall, at the Desire of one fifth of those Present, be entered on the Journal.

Neither House, during the Session of Congress, shall, without the Consent of the other, adjourn for more than three days, nor to any other Place than that in which the two Houses shall be sitting.

Section. 6. The Senators and Representatives shall receive a Compensation for their Services, to be ascertained by Law, and paid out of the Treasury of the United States. They shall in all Cases, except Treason, Felony and Breach of the Peace, be privileged from Arrest during their Attendance at the Session of their respective Houses, and in going to and returning from the same; and for any Speech or Debate in either House, they shall not be questioned in any other Place.

No Senator or Representative shall, during the Time for which he was elected, be appointed to any civil Office under the Authority of the United States, which shall have been created, or the Emoluments whereof shall have been encreased during such time; and no Person holding any Office under the United States, shall be a Member of either House during his Continuance in Office.

Section. 7. All Bills for raising Revenue shall originate in the House of Representatives; but the Senate may propose or concur with Amendments as on other Bills.

~~Every Bill which shall have passed the House of Representatives and the Senate, shall, before it become a Law, be presented to the President of the United States;~~[66] ~~If he approve he shall sign it, but if not he shall return it, with his Objections to that House in which it shall have originated, who shall enter the Objections at large on their Journal, and proceed to reconsider it. If after such Reconsideration two thirds of that House shall agree to pass the Bill, it shall be sent, together with the Objections, to the other House, by which it shall likewise be reconsidered, and if approved by two thirds of that House, it shall become a Law. But in all such Cases the Votes of both Houses shall be determined by yeas and Nays, and the Names of the Persons voting for and against the Bill shall be entered on the Journal of each House respectively. If any Bill shall not be returned by the President within ten Days (Sundays excepted) after it shall have been presented to him, the Same shall be a Law, in like Manner as if he had signed it, unless the Congress by their Adjournment prevent its Return, in which Case it shall not be a Law.~~

[The following proposed Amendment No. 28 changes the above language as follows.]

Every Bill not an appropriation Bill which shall have passed the House of Representatives and the Senate, shall, before it becomes a Law, be presented to the President of the United States. If he approves he shall sign it, but if not he shall return it, with his Objections to the House in which it shall have originated, which shall enter the Objections at large on its Journal, and proceed to reconsider it. If after such Reconsideration two thirds of that House shall agree to pass the Bill, it shall be sent, together with the Objections, to the other House, by which it shall likewise be reconsidered, and if approved by two thirds of that House, it shall

become a Law. Every appropriation Bill which shall have passed the House of Representatives and the Senate shall, before it becomes Law, be presented to the President of the United States; if he approves he shall sign it, but if he approves it in part, he shall sign it as to the sections approved and shall return the Bill with the parts not approved with his Objections to that House in which it shall have originated which shall thereupon proceed in the manner provided for above with respect to Bills which are not appropriation Bills. If the parts objected to are not approved as there provided, such parts shall not be Law but the parts approved shall be Law.[end of proposed language]

Every Order, Resolution, or Vote to which the Concurrence of the Senate and House of Representatives may be necessary (except on a question of Adjournment) shall be presented to the President of the United States; and before the Same shall take Effect, shall be approved by him, or being disapproved by him, shall be repassed by two thirds of the Senate and House of Representatives, according to the Rules and Limitations prescribed in the Case of a Bill.

Section. 8. The Congress shall have Power To lay and collect Taxes, Duties, Imposts and Excises, to pay the Debts and provide for the common Defence and general Welfare of the United States; but all Duties, Imposts and Excises shall be uniform throughout the United States;

To borrow Money on the credit of the United States;

To regulate Commerce with foreign Nations, and among the several States, and with the Indian Tribes;

To establish an uniform Rule of Naturalization, and uniform Laws on the subject of Bankruptcies throughout the United States;

To coin Money, regulate the Value thereof, and of foreign Coin, and fix the Standard of Weights and Measures;

To provide for the Punishment of counterfeiting the Securities and current Coin of the United States;

To establish Post Offices and post Roads;

To promote the Progress of Science and useful Arts, by securing for limited Times to Authors and Inventors the exclusive Right to their respective Writings and Discoveries;

To constitute Tribunals inferior to the supreme Court;

To define and punish Piracies and Felonies committed on the high Seas, and Offences against the Law of Nations;

To declare War, grant Letters of Marque and Reprisal, and make Rules concerning Captures on Land and Water;

To raise and support Armies, but no Appropriation of Money to that Use shall be for a longer Term than two Years;

To provide and maintain a Navy;

To make Rules for the Government and Regulation of the land and naval Forces;

To provide for calling forth the Militia to execute the Laws of the Union, suppress Insurrections and repel Invasions;

To provide for organizing, arming, and disciplining, the Militia, and for governing such Part of them as may be employed in the Service of the United States, reserving to the States respectively, the Appointment of the Officers, and the Authority of training the Militia according to the discipline prescribed by Congress;

To exercise exclusive Legislation in all Cases whatsoever, over such District (not exceeding ten Miles square) as may, by Cession of particular States, and the Acceptance of Congress, become the Seat of the Government of the United States, and to exercise like Authority over all Places purchased by the Consent of the Legislature of the State in which the Same shall be, for the Erection of Forts, Magazines, Arsenals, dock-Yards, and other needful Buildings;—And

To make all Laws which shall be necessary and proper for carrying into Execution the foregoing Powers, and all other Powers vested by this Constitution in the Government of the United States, or in any Department or Officer thereof.

Section. 9. The Migration or Importation of such Persons as any of the States now existing shall think proper to admit, shall not be prohibited by the Congress prior to the Year one thousand eight hundred and eight, but a Tax or duty may be imposed on such Importation, not exceeding ten dollars for each Person.

The Privilege of the Writ of Habeas Corpus shall not be suspended, unless when in Cases of Rebellion or Invasion the public Safety may require it.

No Bill of Attainder or ex post facto Law shall be passed.

No Capitation, or other direct, Tax shall be laid, unless in Proportion to the Census or Enumeration herein before directed to be taken.

No Tax or Duty shall be laid on Articles exported from any State.

No Preference shall be given by any Regulation of Commerce or Revenue to the Ports of one State over those of another; nor shall Vessels bound to, or from, one State, be obliged to enter, clear, or pay Duties in another.

No Money shall be drawn from the Treasury, but in Consequence of Appropriations made by Law; and a regular Statement and Account of the Receipts and Expenditures of all public Money shall be published from time to time.

No Title of Nobility shall be granted by the United States: And no Person holding any Office of Profit or Trust under them, shall, without the Consent of the Congress, accept of any present, Emolument, Office, or Title, of any kind whatever, from any King, Prince, or foreign State.

[The following proposed Amendment No. 29 adds the following seven clauses to Section 9.]

No member of any committee of Congress shall serve on such committee of longer than four terms in the House and two terms in the Senate as those terms are defined in Sections 1 and 2 of Article I of the Constitution.

Any existing Law in conflict with the Twenty Ninth Amendment shall be void except any Law in conflict with Clause 10 of the Twenty Ninth Amendment shall not be void until two years after its adoption during which time Congress shall extinguish all prohibited benefits and pay or promise to pay the present value thereof determined actuarially using a discount rate of ten percent per annum, as of the date of such adoption, to those whose benefits are terminated thereby, with any deferred payment made without interest on such terms and conditions and over such time as Congress shall establish.

Direct and indirect compensation for members of Congress shall be equal. Compensation for members of Congress and their staff shall be established every four years beginning on the first day of the second calendar year following the effective date of the adoption of this amendment by a majority vote of a committee of six, two appointed by Congress, two by the President, and two by a majority vote of the governors of the several States, one each for a term of two years and one each for a term of four years with appointments made in like manner every two years for a term of four years. Committee deadlocks lasting more than thirty days shall be resolved by the President upon application of any committee member. Such committee shall have the power to appropriate from the federal treasury such funds as shall be required to perform its duties including the compensation and expenses of the members thereof which shall be of public record and never exceed for a committee member the amount established for a member of Congress proportionally reduced to his time of actual service. Appropriations to cover all other costs of operating Congress are reserved to Congress.

All Bills and each and every provision thereof or amendment thereto shall be passed by Congress as provided in the Constitution by votes and all votes shall be public, be recorded and be published by voter.

One third of the members of each House shall have the right to have a vote by their House on any Bill whether in committee or not.

Both Houses shall agree on a budget for the succeeding year no later than October 1 of the prior year failing which none of the members thereof shall be qualified to hold elective office in Congress after the expiration of his or her then existing term of office. All future budgets shall be compared to the current year's budget on both a cash and accrual basis and such comparison shall be part of the budget.

No emergency Appropriation Bill whose purpose is to prevent or mitigate or respond to a loss of life or property or a threat to national security shall be valid if it contains any non-emergency spending authorization.

Section. 10. No State shall enter into any Treaty, Alliance, or Confederation; grant Letters of Marque and Reprisal; coin Money; emit Bills of Credit; make any Thing but gold and silver Coin a Tender in Payment of Debts; pass any Bill of Attainder, ex post facto Law, or Law impairing the Obligation of Contracts, or grant any Title of Nobility.

No State shall, without the Consent of the Congress, lay any Imposts or Duties on Imports or Exports, except what may be absolutely necessary for executing it's inspection Laws; and the net Produce of all Duties and Imposts, laid by any State on Imports or Exports, shall be for the Use of the Treasury of the United States; and all such Laws shall be subject to the Revision and Controul of the Congress.

No State shall, without the Consent of Congress, lay any Duty of Tonnage, keep Troops, or Ships of War in time of Peace, enter into any Agreement or Compact with another State, or with a foreign Power, or engage in War, unless actually invaded, or in such imminent Danger as will not admit of delay.

[The following proposed Amendment No. 30 adds the following new section 11.]

Section 11. Congress shall have no power To pass any Bill for raising revenue or for appropriating money unless it is approved by three fifths of both Houses;

To pass any retroactive Bill unless approved by a two thirds vote of both Houses except Congress shall never impose taxes retroactively.

To pass any Bill using its power under the Sixteenth Amendment which is effective before the first day of the calendar year following its enactment without a two thirds vote of both Houses and no such Bill shall ever be made subject to a stated term.

After the adoption of this amendment, To impose an enforceable duty upon State, local or tribal governments or entities by which they do business without their written consent or to discriminate against them in the provision of federal assistance, financial or otherwise, because they refuse to consent.

To pass any Bill limiting the amount of contributions by any United States domiciliary corporation or organization or citizen to any corporation, organization or person for political purposes involving federal policy or federal candidates nor limit the expenditures of any of the foregoing as long as both the contributions and expenditures are fully and promptly disclosed to the public by the most public and technological means available for such purpose.

To pass any Bill unless it sets forth at the beginning thereof a declaration of the purpose thereof and the constitutional power under which it is brought, a statement that the Bill is needed in the public interest, a statement that the government can afford the Bill, a statement that the government can administer the Bill in a way people can respect, a statement of its impact on the freedoms of the citizens and a statement of its possible unintended consequences.

To provide financial assistance to, or purchase any debt securities of, any State or entity by which it does business or subdivisions or municipalities thereof unless the financial assistance or purchase is provided to all States and prorated by population determined by the most recent census or unless approved by a two thirds vote of both Houses.

To exempt itself from any law, or be separately classified so as to be treated differently from the people generally.

To appropriate monies, for any year for which a budget has been established by Congress, a sum greater than one fifth of the gross domestic product of the United States for the prior year as determined by Congress unless the appropriation is approved by a two thirds vote of both Houses.

To pass any Bill conferring a retirement, health, pension or other benefit upon itself or its past, present or future members or any employee of the United States or agency thereof except the military unless such Bill applies generally to all other citizens.

To pass any Bill delegating to the President the authority to take any action subject to Congress' disapproval or to increase spending authority related to any government obligations the budget authority for which has not been provided in advance, unless such delegation is necessary and accompanied by clearly defined and ascertainable standards.

ARTICLE. II.

Section. 1. The executive Power shall be vested in a President of the United States of America. He shall hold his Office during the Term of four Years, and, together with the Vice President, chosen for the same Term, be elected, as follows:

Each State shall appoint, in such Manner as the Legislature thereof may direct, a Number of Electors, equal to the whole Number of Senators and Representatives to which the State may be entitled in the Congress: but no Senator or Representative, or Person holding an Office of Trust or Profit under the United States, shall be appointed an Elector.

The Electors shall meet in their respective States, and vote by Ballot for two Persons, of whom one at least shall not be an Inhabitant of the same State with themselves. And they shall make a List of all the Persons voted for, and of the Number of Votes for each; which List they shall sign and certify, and transmit sealed to the Seat of the Government of the United States, directed to the President of the Senate. The President of the Senate shall, in the Presence of the Senate and House of Representatives, open all the Certificates, and the Votes shall then be counted. The Person having the greatest Number of Votes shall be the President, if such Number be a Majority of the whole Number of Electors appointed; and if there be more than one who have such Majority, and have an equal Number of Votes, then the House of Representatives shall immediately chuse by Ballot one of them for President; and if no Person have a Majority, then from the five highest on the List the said House shall in like Manner chuse the President. But in chusing the President, the Votes shall be taken by States, the Representation from each State having one Vote; a quorum for this Purpose shall consist of a Member or Members from two thirds of the States, and a Majority of all the States shall be necessary to a Choice. In every Case, after the Choice of the President, the Person having the greatest Number of Votes of the Electors shall be the Vice President. But if there should remain two or more who have equal Votes, the Senate shall chuse from them by Ballot the Vice President.[67]

The Congress may determine the Time of chusing the Electors, and the Day on which they shall give their Votes; which Day shall be the same throughout the United States.

No Person except a natural born Citizen, or a Citizen of the United States, at the time of the Adoption of this Constitution, shall be eligible to the Office of President; neither shall any Person be eligible to that Office who shall not have attained to the Age of thirty five Years, and been fourteen Years a Resident within the United States.

In Case of the Removal of the President from Office, or of his Death, Resignation, or Inability to discharge the Powers and Duties of the said Office, the Same shall devolve on the Vice President, and the Congress may by Law provide for the Case of Removal, Death, Resignation or Inability, both of the President and Vice President, declaring what Officer shall then act as President, and such Officer shall act accordingly, until the Disability be removed, or a President shall be elected.[68]

The President shall, at stated Times, receive for his Services, a Compensation, which shall neither be increased nor diminished during the Period for which he shall have been elected, and he shall not receive within that Period any other Emolument from the United States, or any of them.

Before he enter on the Execution of his Office, he shall take the following Oath or Affirmation: "I do solemnly swear (or affirm) that I will faithfully execute the Office of President of the United States, and will to the best of my Ability, preserve, protect and defend the Constitution of the United States."

Section. 2. The President shall be Commander in Chief of the Army and Navy of the United States, and of the Militia of the several States, when called into the actual Service of the United States; he may require the Opinion, in writing, of the principal Officer in each of the executive Departments, upon any Subject relating to the Duties of their respective Offices, and he shall have Power to grant

Reprieves and Pardons for Offences against the United States, except in Cases of Impeachment.

He shall have Power, by and with the Advice and Consent of the Senate, to make Treaties, provided two thirds of the Senators present concur; and he shall nominate, and by and with the Advice and Consent of the Senate, shall appoint Ambassadors, other public Ministers and Consuls, Judges of the supreme Court, and all other Officers of the United States, whose Appointments are not herein otherwise provided for, and which shall be established by Law: but the Congress may by Law vest the Appointment of such inferior Officers, as they think proper, in the President alone, in the Courts of Law, or in the Heads of Departments.

[The following proposed Amendment No. 31 adds the following language to this Section 2.]

The President shall nominate ambassadors, other public ministers and consuls, judges of the Supreme Court and all other federal courts established by Congress upon the advice and consent of the Senate within ninety days of any vacancy and the Senate shall confirm or reject such nomination within one hundred twenty days thereafter whereupon, if the nomination is consented to, the President shall appoint the person so nominated within thirty days. If the President or the Senate, as the case may be, do not timely act, the compensation otherwise payable to the President or members of the Senate and its staff shall be abated without recoupment until such action is taken. [end of proposed language]

The President shall have Power to fill up all Vacancies that may happen during the Recess of the Senate, by granting Commissions which shall expire at the End of their next Session.

Section. 3. He shall from time to time give to the Congress Information of the State of the Union, and recommend to their Consideration such Measures as he shall judge necessary and expedient;

he may, on extraordinary Occasions, convene both Houses, or either of them, and in Case of Disagreement between them, with Respect to the Time of Adjournment, he may adjourn them to such Time as he shall think proper; he shall receive Ambassadors and other public Ministers; he shall take Care that the Laws be faithfully executed, and shall Commission all the Officers of the United States.

Section. 4. The President, Vice President and all civil Officers of the United States, shall be removed from Office on Impeachment for, and Conviction of, Treason, Bribery, or other high Crimes and Misdemeanors.

[The following proposed Amendment No. 32 adds the following five paragraphs to a new Section 5.]

Section 5. All agencies of the federal government having the authority to issue regulations shall receive a priority number by the President by January 1 of each even numbered year with the highest priority being the lowest number. Conflicts among valid regulations among agencies shall be resolved in favor of the agency having the highest priority. New agencies not having a priority number shall have the lowest priority in the order established unless the President amends his prior prioritization.

The delegation of legislative power by Congress to the President or any department or executive agency shall be accompanied by standards and shall be strictly construed. If there is any doubt concerning whether a government official has delegated power, the presumption shall be that he does not. Courts shall not defer to the judgment of legislative or executive officials with respect to their power nor accord to them any presumption of authority but shall require strict proof. Whether any regulation is authorized by law is at any trial a question of fact for the trier of fact though the court can reverse a finding that authority exists if it believes as a matter of law there is no authority. No agency to which legislative power is delegated shall have any privilege to withhold information from Congress.

Except to correct mistakes in regulations which impose greater restrictions on the People than were intended, proposed regulations made by any agency of the United States shall have no effect for any purpose whatsoever until they are adopted and then their effect shall be prospective.

No person shall be required to file an application to obtain a right or permit required by law with more than one agency or department and that agency or department shall coordinate as it deems appropriate with other agencies and departments which have an interest in the matter. If more than one agency or department requires an application for permit, the applicant has the right to select which of the agencies or departments shall receive his application unless otherwise specified by law. Any such application shall be acted upon by the agency or department within one year from the filing thereof or shall thereafter be deemed unconditionally approved as filed. A denial, or approval with conditions which are not satisfied within six months from agency action from the applicant's submission of a satisfaction of conditions, shall be subject to judicial review before the federal court of appeals of the circuit in which the applicant resides.

Upon request of the House of Representatives, the President shall appear before it while in session to answer questions but not more often than weekly and for not more than 40 minutes for each appearance.

ARTICLE. III.

Section. 1. The judicial Power of the United States shall be vested in one supreme Court, and in such inferior Courts as the Congress may from time to time ordain and establish. The Judges, both of the supreme and inferior Courts, shall hold their Offices during good Behaviour, and shall, at stated Times, receive for their Services a Compensation, which shall not be diminished during their Continuance in Office.

Section. 2. The judicial Power shall extend to all Cases, in Law and Equity, arising under this Constitution, the Laws of the United States, and Treaties made, or which shall be made, under their Authority;—to all Cases affecting Ambassadors, other public Ministers and Consuls;—to all Cases of admiralty and maritime Jurisdiction;—to Controversies to which the United States shall be a Party;—to Controversies between two or more States;—between a State and Citizens of another State;[69]—between Citizens of different States;—between Citizens of the same State claiming Lands under Grants of different States, and between a State, or the Citizens thereof, and foreign States, Citizens or Subjects.

In all Cases affecting Ambassadors, other public Ministers and Consuls, and those in which a State shall be Party, the supreme Court shall have original Jurisdiction. In all the other Cases before mentioned, the supreme Court shall have appellate Jurisdiction, both as to Law and Fact, with such Exceptions, and under such Regulations as the Congress shall make.

The Trial of all Crimes, except in Cases of Impeachment, shall be by Jury; and such Trial shall be held in the State where the said Crimes shall have been committed; but when not committed within any State, the Trial shall be at such Place or Places as the Congress may by Law have directed.

Section. 3. Treason against the United States shall consist only in levying War against them, or in adhering to their Enemies, giving them Aid and Comfort. No Person shall be convicted of Treason unless on the Testimony of two Witnesses to the same overt Act, or on Confession in open Court.

The Congress shall have Power to declare the Punishment of Treason, but no Attainder of Treason shall work Corruption of Blood, or Forfeiture except during the Life of the Person attainted.

ARTICLE. IV.

Section. 1. Full Faith and Credit shall be given in each State to the public Acts, Records, and judicial Proceedings of every other State. And the Congress may by general Laws prescribe the Manner in which such Acts, Records and Proceedings shall be proved, and the Effect thereof.

Section. 2. The Citizens of each State shall be entitled to all Privileges and Immunities of Citizens in the several States.

A Person charged in any State with Treason, Felony, or other Crime, who shall flee from Justice, and be found in another State, shall on Demand of the executive Authority of the State from which he fled, be delivered up, to be removed to the State having Jurisdiction of the Crime.

No Person held to Service or Labour in one State, under the Laws thereof, escaping into another, shall, in Consequence of any Law or Regulation therein, be discharged from such Service or Labour, but shall be delivered up on Claim of the Party to whom such Service or Labour may be due.[70]

Section. 3. New States may be admitted by the Congress into this Union; but no new State shall be formed or erected within the Jurisdiction of any other State; nor any State be formed by the Junction of two or more States, or Parts of States, without the Consent of the Legislatures of the States concerned as well as of the Congress.

The Congress shall have Power to dispose of and make all needful Rules and Regulations respecting the Territory or other Property belonging to the United States; and nothing in this Constitution shall be so construed as to Prejudice any Claims of the United States, or of any particular State.

Section. 4. The United States shall guarantee to every State in this Union a Republican Form of Government, and shall protect each of them against Invasion; and on Application of the Legislature, or of the Executive (when the Legislature cannot be convened), against domestic Violence.

ARTICLE. V.

The Congress, whenever two thirds of both Houses shall deem it necessary, shall propose Amendments to this Constitution, or, on the Application of the Legislatures of two thirds of the several States, shall call a Convention for proposing Amendments, which, in either Case, shall be valid to all Intents and Purposes, as Part of this Constitution, when ratified by the Legislatures of three fourths of the several States, or by Conventions in three fourths thereof, as the one or the other Mode of Ratification may be proposed by the Congress; Provided that no Amendment which may be made prior to the Year One thousand eight hundred and eight shall in any Manner affect the first and fourth Clauses in the Ninth Section of the first Article; and that no State, without its Consent, shall be deprived of its equal Suffrage in the Senate.[71]

[The following proposed Amendment No. 33 adds the following two clauses to this Article V.]

Whenever a majority of the legislatures of the several States propose amendments to this Constitution, they shall file the same with Congress which shall within four months return the proposed amendments to the legislatures of the several States with such advice as it deems appropriate and, upon such return or upon the failure of Congress to timely make such return, the proposed amendments, with Congress' return, if any, shall be submitted to the legislatures of the several States and, when ratified by the legislatures of three fourths of the several States, the proposed amendments shall be valid to all intents and purposes according to the provisions thereof.

Any amendment changing the Bill of Rights or the Thirteenth Amendment, Fourteenth Amendment or Fifteenth Amendment shall not be valid unless ratified by all the States.

ARTICLE. VI.

All Debts contracted and Engagements entered into, before the Adoption of this Constitution, shall be as valid against the United States under this Constitution, as under the Confederation.

This Constitution, and the Laws of the United States which shall be made in Pursuance thereof; and all Treaties made, or which shall be made, under the Authority of the United States, shall be the supreme Law of the Land; and the Judges in every State shall be bound thereby, any Thing in the Constitution or Laws of any State to the Contrary notwithstanding.

The Senators and Representatives before mentioned, and the Members of the several State Legislatures, and all executive and judicial Officers, both of the United States and of the several States, shall be bound by Oath or Affirmation, to support this Constitution; but no religious Test shall ever be required as a Qualification to any Office or public Trust under the United States.

[The following proposed Amendment No. 34 adds the following five clauses to this Article VI.]

Notwithstanding Amendment XXIV, as long as the United States obtains revenue under the Sixteenth Amendment, every citizen of the United States eighteen years or older shall file an income tax return and, notwithstanding any other law or provision of this Constitution, make a tax payment equal to the cost of operating Congress divided by the last census of the population of the United States rounded to the nearest dollar but not more than the cost of one fourth troy ounce of silver nor less than ten dollars and, upon payment, shall receive evidence thereof which evidence shall be shown as a condition to the right of such per-

son to vote in any federal election. Such amount until changed by Congress shall be ten dollars and when changed by Congress, shall be published by the President no later than the first business day after January 1 of each even numbered year.

The total size of all regulations issued by all agencies and departments of the United States, measured in bytes of text, shall not exceed four times those contained in all federal statutes; and any regulations in excess of such amount shall be void as of January 1 of each even numbered year in the reverse order of the promulgating agency's priority. No later than November 1 of each odd numbered year, Congress shall publish the bytes of text in all federal statutes effective for the following year and the President shall publish the bytes of text in all regulations of all agencies by priority number for the following year.

Regulations shall be void ten years after they are effective unless earlier approved by Congress for a stated term. Congress shall have the authority to exempt specified regulations from this provision.

Unless increased by a majority vote of the State legislatures upon the request of Congress, the total staff answerable to each member of the House of Representatives and Senate and their committees shall not exceed 25,000 persons for allocation among them as the members of Congress deem appropriate.

No person in government, elected, hired or appointed, shall suppress any information relating to the sighting or existence of extra-terrestrial phenomena and shall have a duty to preserve and disclose any such information to the public promptly as it becomes available including information existing at the time of the adoption of this amendment.

ARTICLE. VII.

The Ratification of the Conventions of nine States, shall be sufficient for the Establishment of this Constitution between the States so ratifying the Same.

The Word, "the," being interlined between the seventh and eighth Lines of the first Page, The Word "Thirty" being partly written on an Erazure in the fifteenth Line of the first Page, The Words "is tried" being interlined between the thirty second and thirty third Lines of the first Page and the Word "the" being interlined between the forty third and forty fourth Lines of the second Page.

Attest William Jackson

Secretary

done in Convention by the Unanimous Consent of the States present the Seventeenth Day of September in the Year of our Lord one thousand seven hundred and Eighty seven and of the Independence of the United States of America the Twelfth In witness whereof We have hereunto subscribed our Names,

Go. Washington—Presidt.
and deputy from Virginia

New Hampshire
    John Langdon
    Nicholas Gilman
Massachusetts
    Nathaniel Gorham
    Rufus King
Connecticut
    Wm. Saml. Johnson
    Roger Sherman
New York
    Alexander Hamilton

New Jersey
    Wil: Livingston
    David Brearley.
    Wm. Paterson.
    Jona: Dayton
Pennsylvania
    B Franklin
    Thomas Mifflin
    Robt Morris
    Geo. Clymer
    Thos. Fitz Simons
    Jared Ingersoll
    James Wilson
    Gouv Morris

Delaware
    Geo: Read
    Gunning Bedford jun
    John Dickinson
    Richard Bassett
    Jaco: Broom
Maryland
    James McHenry
    Dan of St Thos. Jenifer
    Danl Carroll
Virginia
    John Blair
    James Madison

North Carolina
    Wm. Blount
    Richd. Dobbs Spaight
    Hu Williamson
South Carolina
    J. Rutledge
    Charles Cotesworth Pinckney
    Charles Pinckney
    Pierce Butler
Georgia
    William Few
    Abr Baldwin

In Convention Monday, September 17th, 1787.

Present

The States of

New Hampshire, Massachusetts, Connecticut, Mr. Hamilton from New York, New Jersey, Pennsylvania, Delaware, Maryland, Virginia, North Carolina, South Carolina and Georgia.

Resolved,

That the preceeding Constitution be laid before the United States in Congress assembled, and that it is the Opinion of this Convention, that it should afterwards be submitted to a Convention of Delegates, chosen in each State by the People thereof, under the Recommendation of its Legislature, for their Assent and Ratification; and that each Convention assenting to, and ratifying the Same, should give Notice thereof to the United States in Congress assembled. Resolved, That it is the Opinion of this Convention, that as soon as the Conventions of nine States shall have ratified this Constitution, the United States in Congress assembled should fix a Day on which Electors should be appointed by the States which have ratified the same, and a Day on which the Electors should assemble to vote for the President, and the Time and Place for commencing Proceedings under this Constitution. That after such Publication the Electors should be appointed, and the Senators and Representatives elected: That the Electors should meet on the Day fixed for the Election of the President, and should transmit their Votes certified, signed, sealed and directed, as the Constitution requires, to the Secretary of the United States in Congress assembled, that the Senators and Representatives should convene at the Time and Place assigned; that the Senators should appoint a President of the Senate, for the sole purpose of receiving, opening and counting the Votes for President; and, that after he shall be chosen, the Congress, together with the President, should, without Delay, proceed to execute this Constitution.

By the Unanimous Order of the Convention

Go. Washington—Presidt.

W. Jackson Secretary.

The Bill of Rights:
The Preamble to The Bill of Rights
Congress of the United States
begun and held at the City of New-York,
on Wednesday the fourth of March,
one thousand seven hundred and eighty nine

THE Conventions of a number of the States, having at the time of their adopting the Constitution, expressed a desire, in order to prevent misconstruction or abuse of its powers, that further declaratory and restrictive clauses should be added: And as extending the ground of public confidence in the Government, will best ensure the beneficent ends of its institution.

RESOLVED by the Senate and House of Representatives of the United States of America, in Congress assembled, two thirds of both

Houses concurring, that the following Articles be proposed to the Legislatures of the several States, as amendments to the Constitution of the United States, all, or any of which Articles, when ratified by three fourths of the said Legislatures, to be valid to all intents and purposes, as part of the said Constitution; viz.

ARTICLES in addition to, and Amendment of the Constitution of the United States of America, proposed by Congress, and ratified by the Legislatures of the several States, pursuant to the fifth Article of the original Constitution.

Note: The following text is a transcription of the first ten amendments to the Constitution in their original form. These amendments were ratified December 15, 1791, and form what is known as the "Bill of Rights."

AMENDMENT I.

Congress shall make no law respecting an establishment of religion, or prohibiting the free exercise thereof; or abridging the freedom of speech, or of the press; or the right of the people peaceably to assemble, and to petition the Government for a redress of grievances.

AMENDMENT II.

A well regulated Militia, being necessary to the security of a free State, the right of the people to keep and bear Arms, shall not be infringed.

AMENDMENT III.

No Soldier shall, in time of peace be quartered in any house, without the consent of the Owner, nor in time of war, but in a manner to be prescribed by law.

AMENDMENT IV.

The right of the people to be secure in their persons, houses, papers, and effects, against unreasonable searches and seizures, shall not be violated, and no Warrants shall issue, but upon probable cause, supported by Oath or affirmation, and particularly describing the place to be searched, and the persons or things to be seized.

AMENDMENT V.

No person shall be held to answer for a capital, or otherwise infamous crime, unless on a presentment or indictment of a Grand Jury, except in cases arising in the land or naval forces, or in the Militia, when in actual service in time of War or public danger; nor shall any person be subject for the same offence to be twice put in jeopardy of life or limb; nor shall be compelled in any criminal case to be a witness against himself, nor be deprived of life, liberty, or property, without due process of law; nor shall private property be taken for public use, without just compensation.

AMENDMENT VI.

In all criminal prosecutions, the accused shall enjoy the right to a speedy and public trial, by an impartial jury of the State and district wherein the crime shall have been committed, which district shall have been previously ascertained by law, and to be informed of the nature and cause of the accusation; to be confronted with the witnesses against him; to have compulsory process for obtaining witnesses in his favor, and to have the Assistance of Counsel for his defence.

AMENDMENT VII.

In Suits at common law, where the value in controversy shall exceed twenty dollars, the right of trial by jury shall be preserved, and no fact tried by a jury, shall be otherwise re-examined in any Court of the United States, than according to the rules of the common law.

AMENDMENT VIII.

Excessive bail shall not be required, nor excessive fines imposed, nor cruel and unusual punishments inflicted.

AMENDMENT IX.

The enumeration in the Constitution, of certain rights, shall not be construed to deny or disparage others retained by the people.

AMENDMENT X.

~~The powers not delegated to the United States by the Constitution, nor prohibited by it to the States, are reserved to the States respectively, or to the people.~~

[The following proposed Amendment No. 35 revises Amendment X as follows.]

Section 1. The powers not delegated to the United States by the Constitution, nor prohibited by it to the States, are reserved to the States respectively, or to the people. Such powers shall include all those powers not expressly delegated to Congress under the Constitution whether or not those powers existed prior to the adoption of the Constitution or those arising thereafter as a result of the Constitution. The States shall not exercise these powers in a way which diminishes or interferes with the powers expressly delegated by the Constitution to Congress, the President or the Judiciary.

Section 2. The legislature of each State shall have the power to limit the terms of the Senators and Representatives in Congress representing such State.

Section 3. The legislatures of two thirds of the several States shall have the power to repeal any law or part thereof or regulation of the United States or remove any federal judge or justice of the Supreme Court by a resolution describing the law or part thereof or regulation to be repealed or judge or justice to be removed with the effective date of such action being as stated in the resolution or upon obtaining the required approval whichever date is later. Upon the required approval, the resolution shall be signed by the governors of the states having the approving legislatures, shall contain a certification of approval and shall be delivered to the President and Congress by the governor last to sign and shall take effect as provided therein.

Section 4. There is hereby established a Board of Governors whose members shall be the governors of the several States which shall act according to rules adopted by the governors of the several States. The Board of Governors shall have power by a two thirds vote of its members to make recommendations to Congress or to their State legislatures and to administer all activities assigned to the States or State legislatures herein as they deem in the best interests of the United States. The Board of Governors shall be immune from all taxes.

Section 5. Any approval by the legislatures of the States as used in the Constitution means approval by a majority of all members of each House in their legislative branch.

[Following are constitutional Amendments XI through XXVII]
AMENDMENT XI.

Passed by Congress March 4, 1794. Ratified February 7, 1795.
Note: Article III, section 2, of the Constitution was modified by amendment 11.

The Judicial power of the United States shall not be construed to extend to any suit in law or equity, commenced or prosecuted against one of the United States by Citizens of another State, or by Citizens or Subjects of any Foreign State.

AMENDMENT XII.

Passed by Congress December 9, 1803. Ratified June 15, 1804.
Note: A portion of Article II, section 1 of the Constitution was superseded by the 12th amendment.

The Electors shall meet in their respective states and vote by ballot for President and Vice-President, one of whom, at least, shall not be an inhabitant of the same state with themselves; they shall name in their ballots the person voted for as President, and in distinct ballots the person voted for as Vice-President, and they shall make distinct lists of all persons voted for as President, and of all persons voted for as Vice-President, and of the number of votes for each, which lists they shall sign and certify, and transmit sealed to the seat of the government of the United States, directed to the President of the Senate;—the President of the Senate shall, in the presence of the Senate and House of Representatives, open all the certificates and the votes shall then be counted;—The person having the greatest number of votes for President, shall be the President, if such number be a majority of the whole number of Electors appointed; and if no person have such majority, then from the persons having the highest numbers not exceeding three on the list of those voted for as President, the House of Representatives shall choose immediately, by ballot, the President. But in choosing the President, the votes shall be taken by states, the representation from each state having one vote; a quorum for this purpose shall consist of a member or members from two-thirds of the states, and a majority of all the states shall be necessary to a choice. [And if the House of Representatives shall not choose a President whenever the right of choice shall devolve upon them, before the fourth day of March next following, then the Vice-President shall act as President, as in case of the death or other constitutional disability of the President.—]* The person having the greatest number of votes as Vice-President, shall be the Vice-President, if such number be a majority of the whole number of Electors appointed, and if no person have a majority, then from the two highest numbers on the list, the Senate shall choose the Vice-President; a quorum for the purpose shall consist of two-thirds of the whole number of Senators, and a majority of the whole number shall be necessary to a choice. But no person constitutionally ineligible to the office of President shall be eligible to that of Vice-President of the United States.

*Superseded by section 3 of the 20th amendment.

AMENDMENT XIII.

Passed by Congress January 31, 1865. Ratified December 6, 1865.
Note: A portion of Article IV, section 2, of the Constitution was superseded by the 13th amendment.

Section 1. Neither slavery nor involuntary servitude, except as a punishment for crime whereof the party shall have been duly convicted, shall exist within the United States, or any place subject to their jurisdiction.

Section 2. Congress shall have power to enforce this article by appropriate legislation.

AMENDMENT XIV.

Passed by Congress June 13, 1866. Ratified July 9, 1868.
Note: Article I, section 2, of the Constitution was modified by section 2 of the 14th amendment.

Section 1. All persons born or naturalized in the United States, and subject to the jurisdiction thereof, are citizens of the United States and of the State wherein they reside. No State shall make or enforce any law which shall abridge the privileges or immunities of citizens of the United States; nor shall any State deprive any person of life, liberty, or property, without due process of law; nor deny to any person within its jurisdiction the equal protection of the laws.

Section 2. Representatives shall be apportioned among the several States according to their respective numbers, counting the whole number of persons in each State, excluding Indians not taxed. But when the right to vote at any election for the choice of electors for President and Vice-President of the United States, Representatives in Congress, the Executive and Judicial officers of a State, or the members of the Legislature thereof, is denied to any of the male inhabitants of such State, being twenty-one years of age,* and citizens of the United States, or in any way abridged, except for participation in rebellion, or other crime, the basis of representation therein shall be reduced in the proportion which the number of such male citizens shall bear to the whole number of male citizens twenty-one years of age in such State.

Section 3. No person shall be a Senator or Representative in Congress, or elector of President and Vice-President, or hold any office, civil or military, under the United States, or under any State, who, having previously taken an oath, as a member of Congress, or as an officer of the United States, or as a member of any State legislature, or as an executive or judicial officer of any State, to support the Constitution of the United States, shall have engaged in insurrection or rebellion against the same, or given aid or comfort to the enemies thereof. But Congress may by a vote of two-thirds of each House, remove such disability.

Section 4. The validity of the public debt of the United States, authorized by law, including debts incurred for payment of pensions and bounties for services in suppressing insurrection or rebellion, shall not be questioned. But neither the United States nor any State shall assume or pay any debt or obligation incurred in aid of insurrection or rebellion against the United States, or any claim for the loss or emancipation of any slave; but all such debts, obligations and claims shall be held illegal and void.

Section 5. The Congress shall have the power to enforce, by appropriate legislation, the provisions of this article.
Changed by section 1 of the 26th amendment.

AMENDMENT XV.

Passed by Congress February 26, 1869. Ratified February 3, 1870.

Section 1. The right of citizens of the United States to vote shall not be denied or abridged by the United States or by any State on account of race, color, or previous condition of servitude--

Section 2. The Congress shall have the power to enforce this article by appropriate legislation.

AMENDMENT XVI.

Passed by Congress July 2, 1909. Ratified February 3, 1913.

Note: Article I, section 9, of the Constitution was modified by amendment 16.

The Congress shall have power to lay and collect taxes on incomes, from whatever source derived, without apportionment among the several States, and without regard to any census or enumeration.

AMENDMENT XVII.

Passed by Congress May 13, 1912. Ratified April 8, 1913.

Note: Article I, section 3, of the Constitution was modified by the 17th amendment.

The Senate of the United States shall be composed of two Senators from each State, elected by the people thereof, for six years; and each Senator shall have one vote. The electors in each State shall have the qualifications requisite for electors of the most numerous branch of the State legislatures.

When vacancies happen in the representation of any State in the Senate, the executive authority of such State shall issue writs of election to fill such vacancies: *Provided*, That the legislature of any State may empower the executive thereof to make temporary appointments until the people fill the vacancies by election as the legislature may direct.

This amendment shall not be so construed as to affect the election or term of any Senator chosen before it becomes valid as part of the Constitution.

AMENDMENT XVIII.

Passed by Congress December 18, 1917. Ratified January 16, 1919. Repealed by amendment 21.

Section 1. After one year from the ratification of this article the manufacture, sale, or transportation of intoxicating liquors within, the importation thereof into, or the exportation thereof from the United States and all territory subject to the jurisdiction thereof for beverage purposes is hereby prohibited.

Section 2. The Congress and the several States shall have concurrent power to enforce this article by appropriate legislation.

Section 3. This article shall be inoperative unless it shall have been ratified as an amendment to the Constitution by the legislatures of the several States, as provided in the Constitution, within seven years from the date of the submission hereof to the States by the Congress.

AMENDMENT XIX.

Passed by Congress June 4, 1919. Ratified August 18, 1920.

The right of citizens of the United States to vote shall not be denied or abridged by the United States or by any State on account of sex.

Congress shall have power to enforce this article by appropriate legislation.

AMENDMENT XX.

Passed by Congress March 2, 1932. Ratified January 23, 1933.

Note: Article I, section 4, of the Constitution was modified by section 2 of this amendment. In addition, a portion of the 12th amendment was superseded by section 3.

Section 1. The terms of the President and the Vice President shall end at noon on the 20th day of January, and the terms of Senators and Representatives at noon on the 3d day of January, of the years in which such terms would have ended if this article had not been ratified; and the terms of their successors shall then begin.

Section 2. The Congress shall assemble at least once in every year, and such meeting shall begin at noon on the 3d day of January, unless they shall by law appoint a different day.

Section 3. If, at the time fixed for the beginning of the term of the President, the President elect shall have died, the Vice President elect shall become President. If a President shall not have been chosen before the time fixed for the beginning of his term, or if the President elect shall have failed to qualify, then the Vice President elect shall act as President until a President shall have qualified; and the Congress may by law provide for the case wherein neither a President elect nor a Vice President shall have qualified, declaring who shall then act as President, or the manner in which one who is to act shall be selected, and such person shall act accordingly until a President or Vice President shall have qualified.

Section 4. The Congress may by law provide for the case of the death of any of the persons from whom the House of Representatives may choose a President whenever the right of choice shall have devolved upon them, and for the case of the death of any of the persons from whom the Senate may choose a Vice President whenever the right of choice shall have devolved upon them.

Section 5. Sections 1 and 2 shall take effect on the 15th day of October following the ratification of this article.

Section 6. This article shall be inoperative unless it shall have been ratified as an amendment to the Constitution by the legislatures of three-fourths of the several States within seven years from the date of its submission.

AMENDMENT XXI.

Passed by Congress February 20, 1933. Ratified December 5, 1933.

Section 1. The eighteenth article of amendment to the Constitution of the United States is hereby repealed.

Section 2. The transportation or importation into any State, Territory, or Possession of the United States for delivery or use therein of intoxicating liquors, in violation of the laws thereof, is hereby prohibited.

Section 3. This article shall be inoperative unless it shall have been ratified as an amendment to the Constitution by conventions in the several States, as provided in the Constitution, within seven years from the date of the submission hereof to the States by the Congress.

AMENDMENT XXII.

Passed by Congress March 21, 1947. Ratified February 27, 1951.

Section 1. No person shall be elected to the office of the President more than twice, and no person who has held the office of President, or acted as President, for more than two years of a term to which some other person was elected President shall be elected to the office of President more than once. But this Article shall not apply to any person holding the office of President when this Article was proposed by Congress, and shall not prevent any person who may be holding the office of President, or acting as President, during the term within which this Article becomes operative from holding the office of President or acting as President during the remainder of such term.

Section 2. This article shall be inoperative unless it shall have been ratified as an amendment to the Constitution by the legislatures of three-fourths of the several States within seven years from the date of its submission to the States by the Congress.

AMENDMENT XXIII.

Passed by Congress June 16, 1960. Ratified March 29, 1961.

Section 1. The District constituting the seat of Government of the United States shall appoint in such manner as Congress may direct:

A number of electors of President and Vice President equal to the whole number of Senators and Representatives in Congress to which the District would be entitled if it were a State, but in no event more than the least populous State; they shall be in addition to those appointed by the States, but they shall be considered, for the purposes of the election of President and Vice President, to be electors appointed by a State; and they shall meet in the District and perform such duties as provided by the twelfth article of amendment.

Section 2. The Congress shall have power to enforce this article by appropriate legislation.

AMENDMENT XXIV.

Passed by Congress August 27, 1962. Ratified January 23, 1964.

Section 1. The right of citizens of the United States to vote in any primary or other election for President or Vice President, for electors for President or Vice President, or for Senator or Representative in Congress, shall not be denied or abridged by the United States or any State by reason of failure to pay poll tax or other tax.

Section 2. The Congress shall have power to enforce this article by appropriate legislation.

AMENDMENT XXV.

Passed by Congress July 6, 1965. Ratified February 10, 1967.
Note: Article II, section 1, of the Constitution was affected by the 25th amendment.

Section 1. In case of the removal of the President from office or of his death or resignation, the Vice President shall become President.

Section 2. Whenever there is a vacancy in the office of the Vice President, the President shall nominate a Vice President who shall take office upon confirmation by a majority vote of both Houses of Congress.

Section 3. Whenever the President transmits to the President pro tempore of the Senate and the Speaker of the House of Representatives his written declaration that he is unable to discharge the powers and duties of his office, and until he transmits to them a written declaration to the contrary, such powers and duties shall be discharged by the Vice President as Acting President.

Section 4. Whenever the Vice President and a majority of either the principal officers of the executive departments or of such other body as Congress may by law provide, transmit to the President pro tempore of the Senate and the Speaker of the House of Representatives their written declaration that the President is unable to discharge the powers and duties of his office, the Vice President shall immediately assume the powers and duties of the office as Acting President.

Thereafter, when the President transmits to the President pro tempore of the Senate and the Speaker of the House of Representatives his written declaration that no inability exists, he shall resume the powers and duties of his office unless the Vice President and a majority of either the principal officers of the executive department or of such other body as Congress may by law provide, transmit within four days to the President pro tempore of the Senate and the

Speaker of the House of Representatives their written declaration that the President is unable to discharge the powers and duties of his office. Thereupon Congress shall decide the issue, assembling within forty-eight hours for that purpose if not in session. If the Congress, within twenty-one days after receipt of the latter written declaration, or, if Congress is not in session, within twenty-one days after Congress is required to assemble, determines by two-thirds vote of both Houses that the President is unable to discharge the powers and duties of his office, the Vice President shall continue to discharge the same as Acting President; otherwise, the President shall resume the powers and duties of his office.

AMENDMENT XXVI.

Passed by Congress March 23, 1971. Ratified July 1, 1971.
Note: Amendment 14, section 2, of the Constitution was modified by section 1 of the 26th amendment.

Section 1. The right of citizens of the United States, who are eighteen years of age or older, to vote shall not be denied or abridged by the United States or by any State on account of age.

Section 2. The Congress shall have power to enforce this article by appropriate legislation.

AMENDMENT XXVII.

Originally proposed Sept. 25, 1789. Ratified May 7, 1992.

No law, varying the compensation for the services of the Senators and Representatives, shall take effect, until an election of representatives shall have intervened.

For a recitation of proposed Amendments Nos. 28–36, which have been incorporated into the Constitution above, please see Appendix D.

Footnotes to the Constitution without regard to proposed amendments.

60. The title was not a part of the original document. It was added when the document was printed.

61. Section numbers are not in the original document. We have added them here without putting all of them in brackets.

62. Modified by Amendment XIV.

63. Modified by Amendment XVII.

64. Modified by Amendment XVII.

65. Modified by Amendment XX.

66. Our scanned images show this as a semi-colon, but an image at a congressional site shows a comma.

67. Modified by Amendment XII.

68. Modified by Amendment XXV.

69. Modified by Amendment XI.

70. Modified by Amendment XIII.

71. Possibly abrogated by Amendment XVII.

BUSINESS PLAN

CAMPAIGN CONSTITUTION BUSINESS PLAN

MISSION

To preserve our freedom by limiting the power of Congress with process amendments to the Constitution, originated and ratified by the States without the discretionary participation of Congress, which will encourage the election of leaders who have the virtue and courage to be statesmen.

1. Purpose

The purpose of Campaign Constitution (CC) is to effectuate process amendments to the United States Constitution. Process amendments are amendments that relate to procedures and methods by which decision makers are selected, serve, and make decisions and are thereby only indirectly related to public policies that affect our country on a day-to-day basis. More importantly, people who will differ greatly on public policy issues can nonetheless agree on process amendments. That process amendments transcend political affiliation and those other touchstones that divide our citizenry on most material issues is confirmed by many political scientists. Nobel Laureate F. A. Hayek said:

> ...while agreement is not possible on most of the particular ends which will not be known except to those who pursue them...agreement on means can to a great extent be achieved precisely because it is not known which particular ends they will serve.

For the foregoing reasons, by effectuating process amendments, we receive different decision makers with different values who we hope will be better decision makers and give us both meaningful and desirable changes and thereby better public policy and increased respect for our system of government.

2. Need for Process Amendments

If one thing is clear in the commentary on American politics, it is that most citizens on the subject of the performance of the United States Congress have a negative opinion.

Whether we like it or not, our federal government has evolved from early traditions of setting standards and providing for the common defense to promoting welfare through policies of redistribution. Apart from the many risks associated with the planning behind redistribution programs, the growth of regulations needed to manage these policies portends major risks to our freedoms, rule of law, and respect for our institutions.

The growth of laws and regulations has substantially destroyed the principle of legality, which has been the cornerstone of our political and economic freedom. The uncertainty generated by a growing mass of laws and regulations ever increasing in their conflict with each other has caused us to drift to a country ruled by men and not by law. It is not surprising that, as this phenomenon develops, individual members of Congress and important federal servants become necessary to the accomplishment of progress. This in turn explains the growth of lobbyists and vested interests that seek favors from public servants in the particular distribution process in which they are interested.

That this state of affairs should not be so is illustrated by the history that precedes the fall of all civilizations. While we may not be able to insulate ourselves from the certain fate of decay that befalls civilizations, at one time or another, we can do our best to delay that day of reckoning, to continue the ideals that have made this country strong and free, and, to the extent possible, to restore principle and integrity to national policy in the hope that wise judges and good congressmen can re-engage the rule of law that has been the hallmark of our country. Not less important than rule of law is the need for leaders who have the discipline and courage to resist the temptations of short-term demands in exchange for a proper balance between the competing demands of short-term and long-term objectives.

We believe CC, if properly funded, organized, and managed, can be effective in amending the United States Constitution in a manner that will improve our government and meet the goals set forth above.

3. Structure

CC is a Colorado nonprofit corporation seeking qualification under Section 501(c)(4) of the Internal Revenue Code because its purpose is promoting the general welfare of the people. Initially, it is managed by John M. Cogswell, who will seek advice from an Advisory Committee. As time progresses, the Advisory Committee will expand to fifteen (15) persons selected on a nonpartisan basis for their interest in and understanding of the Constitution and its history.

4. Policies

The policies of CC shall be established by Mr. Cogswell after advice from the Advisory Committee.

5. Amendments to the U.S. Constitution

Article V of the U.S. Constitution states:

> The Congress, whenever two-thirds of both Houses shall deem it necessary, shall propose Amendments to this Constitution, or, on the Application of the Legislatures of two-thirds of the several States, shall call a Convention for proposing Amendments, which, in either Case, shall be valid to all Intents and Purposes, as Part of this Constitution, when ratified by the Legislatures of three-fourths of the several States, or by Conventions in three-fourths thereof, as the one or the other Mode of Ratification may be proposed by the Congress....

This article permits amendments to the U.S. Constitution in two ways:

The first and more traditional method is for Congress, by two-thirds of both houses, to propose amendments and then to specify the manner by which they shall be ratified by the States, that is either by the legislatures of three-fourths of the States or by conventions of three-fourths of the States.

The second method is for two-thirds of the legislatures of the States to apply to the Congress for the calling of a convention for proposing amendments. The amendments resulting from such convention must thereupon be approved by three-fourths of the State legislatures or three-fourths of the conventions convened by the State legislatures as may be proposed by Congress. While States have the initiative to propose amendments under this method, Congress continues to have some ability to influence the process through the two decisions it must make, namely the calling of a convention and the specifying of the mode of ratification. With respect to these two decisions, Congress's obligation to call a convention is mandatory as evidenced by the use of the word "shall," though its decision as to the mode of ratification (approval of three-fourths of the States or approval at a convention) is probably discretionary as evidenced by the use of the words "may be proposed." Congress has traditionally selected State ratification, and a convention has never been called.

CC intends to achieve its process amendments by the second method and to facilitate their enactment by coordinating with all of the State legislatures for the purpose of developing proposed amendments that are identical in form and that specify as a part thereof the procedures to be utilized at the constitutional convention. One will recall that balance-the-budget amendments have periodically failed in part because of media and other public hysteria, raising fears that a constitutional convention would open the door to wholesale changes to all provisions of the Constitution. In order to avert this type of hysteria, CC intends to include as part of the rules of the convention a germaneness provision limiting the power of the convention to the subjects approved by the States.

6. Selection of Process Amendments

CC's Articles of Incorporation provide that CC will support only those process amendments approved by its Advisory Committee and supported by a substantial number of all Americans as evidenced by appropriate polling activities. CC's goal is to support amendments that most any American would agree with and support.

7. Process Amendments

Mr. Cogswell has prepared and submitted forty-four proposed amendments. He has no expectation that there will be general bipartisan agreement on all of these and anticipates that revisions, deletions, and additions will occur based on activities of CC and its Advisory Committee. These forty-four proposed amendments are set forth in a proposed Constitutional Convention Resolution. Mr. Cogswell has written a separate commentary on each proposal, in addition to twelve essays on subjects believed by him to be important to the understanding of his values.

8. Action Plan

CC's action plan will be divided into four phases as follows:

Phase 1: *Pre-Funding Phase*

(1) Select one or more of the finest constitutional scholars available to guide it in its amendment drafting process.

(2) Obtain funds sufficient to host and operate a website and publish a book including the information therein. All rights to the book will be assigned to CC to help fund its activities.

(3) Identify and appoint all members of the Advisory Committee.

(4) Adopt a detailed budget and management plan for organizing each State to support adoption of the proposed amendments.

Phase 2: *Post-Funding and Mock Constitutional Convention*

(1) CC will hire necessary personnel initially consisting of a business manager, a public relations consultant, a fundraising specialist, a financial consultant, and field representatives.

(2) The fifty States will be divided into separate areas and allocated to field representatives who will thereupon identify the key political representatives of both parties in their respective States. These persons are expected to be the leaders of both Houses and any others identified as influential and persuasive with respect to legislative action in the State.

(3) The proposed amendments, as modified by the advice of the Advisory Committee, shall be tested in the polls and filtered by the bipartisan standards established by CC.

(4) The amendments selected for initial action will be drafted and circulated for comment to the legislative representatives selected in the States.

(5) The amendments will be revised following the comment period as appropriate.

(6) A meeting ("Mock Convention") of the legislative representatives will be hosted by CC at a central location.

(7) The Mock Convention shall (i) debate the amendments and vote upon them and (ii) outline the general strategy for obtaining approval by the respective State legislatures. At this time, an action plan shall be adopted, including dates for bill submissions, sponsors, and community action.

(8) CC shall search out and identify a parliamentarian of impeccable credentials who has studied and is familiar with both the procedures employed at the original Constitutional Convention in 1787 and the rules of the Houses of Congress and such person shall be retained to write the rules for the anticipated Constitutional Convention.

(9) The resolution to be submitted to each State legislature for approval shall condition that legislature's support of the process amendments on adherence to specified parliamentary rules, which will be set forth in the amendment which rules shall contain a provision on germaneness designed to preclude consideration of any aspect of the Constitution not germane to the specific process amendments recommended.

(10) Efforts will be taken to cause at least two-thirds of the State legislators to approve an application to Congress containing the amendments and seeking a Constitutional Convention.

(11) Research and support will be provided to the States with respect to their State law procedures for electing delegates to the Constitutional Convention.

(12) Changes to CC's website shall be made as necessary to support the foregoing activities.

Phase 3: *Constitutional Convention*

(1) When two-thirds of the State legislatures approve the application to Congress with the approved amendments, a Constitutional Convention convened by order of the Congress shall be held and the convention procedures established.

(2) The Constitutional Convention will be held and report the amendments adopted to Congress.

(3) Congress has a duty to refer the amendments to the legislatures of the States or to conventions of the States for approval by three-fourths of the States or conventions.

Phase 4: *Post Constitutional Convention*

(1) CC will support efforts to ratify the amendments by the States by their legislatures or convention, as Congress specifies, through public appearances, seminars, and electronic communications.

9. Scheduling

A schedule shall be established to satisfy CC's objectives as quickly as possible.

10. Future Process Amendments

CC, having achieved its initial goal in amending the Constitution, will continually explore recommendations to improve our system of government by process changes to the United States Constitution satisfying applicable standards and support them in the future in a manner similar to that set forth above. It is anticipated that CC could become a major force in American politics by organizing States in a manner that can make them effective as a counter deterrent to the current practices of the United States Congress, which are almost universally condemned by all responsible citizens. The overall effect would be to make Congress more responsible by electing more responsible congressmen and senators and reminding them continually that the United States is a confederation of States and their citizens, with the people having the greatest power and wisdom to guide the direction of our country.

D

CONSTITUTIONAL CONVENTION RESOLUTION

PREAMBLE

When in the course of human events it becomes necessary for the people to reform the political bands that have connected them with one another to secure their liberties, a decent respect for the opinions of mankind requires that they should unite and take the action necessary to do this.

These liberties, first documented for us by the Declaration of Independence, are evidenced by our Constitution, which established new political bands to secure for us certain self-evident and unalienable rights, including Life, Liberty, and the Pursuit of Happiness. Yet, we observe that our government has become destructive to these ends, thereby igniting our right to rearrange the bands that connect us to each other by laying on their foundations principles of harmony and reverence, by restoring a proper allocation of powers intended by the Constitution, and by supplying the methods of government most likely to secure these liberties for ourselves and our posterity.

Prudence dictates that governments long established should not be changed for light and transient causes, but experience has shown that we are more disposed to suffer evils than to right ourselves by abolishing them. However, when a long train of abuses and usurpations have infected our political bands and replaced our unalienable rights with vested interests, national bankruptcy, demagoguery, and a disregard for our future as a nation, it is our right and duty to reform the political bands of our government to provide new guards for our liberties and future security.

Such has been our patient suffering that it is now necessary that we reform these bands and repair the broken system of our government to remedy its repeated injuries, usurpations, and insults, which inevitably have as their direct consequence the establishment of tyranny over us and our States. To prove this, let facts be submitted to a candid nation that those who manage our federal government have:

- Violated their sacred trust to put the nation's interests above their own.
- Relied on pundits irresponsibly and without account instead of common sense.
- Mismanaged the finances of the nation and wasted public monies.
- Misled the people as to the truth of our national condition.
- Used their offices to achieve personal advantages at the expense of the public.
- Imposed obligations on the States without their consent.
- Passed laws without reading them.
- Created agencies with a morass of regulations, which undermine the rule of law.
- Exploited human nature by using the media to distort the truth and raise unjustified expectations.
- Distorted those political bands that made our country great by passing laws and regulations that have reduced regulations, competition, property rights, thrift, creativity, and the work ethic.

We, therefore, the States of the United States of America, in convention duly assembled, appeal to the people to cause their States to ratify these amendments to the Constitution and, for the support of this declaration and with a firm reliance on the protection of Divine Providence, resolve as follows:

RESOLUTION

WHEREAS we the States of the United States have determined that forces not in effect in 1787 have come about and now operate in a manner that impede our ability to elect senators and representatives to the Congress who can properly and efficiently represent our common interests and among these forces are those of vested interests, incumbency, careerism, self-interest, procedural rules of Congress, polling, uninformed television, lack of virtue, and a misplaced understanding of public interest and the role of freedom in our society; and

WHEREAS the specific effects of these forces are to cause our national interest to be subordinate to the self-interests of elected representatives, to cause the relevant facts upon which public policy is made to be misrepresented to us, to give influence to irreverent democratic forces that undo the benefits of a republic, to encourage demagoguery to permit the election of persons whose character is inferior to that of the Founding Fathers and generally to cause principle to be subordinate to expediency; and

WHEREAS the result of these effects is that persons are elected who have an improper influence over the course of our country, which results in decisions that diminish the benefits of our form of government, which abuse and betray the trust under which our elected leaders took office and which erode our freedoms; and

WHEREAS two-thirds of the States of the United States have determined it appropriate to amend the U.S. Constitution on the terms and according to the procedures contained herein;

NOW THEREFORE, we the undersigned States acting by our governors, by reason of resolutions duly adopted by two-thirds of our State legislatures, do hereby ordain and establish that there shall be convened according to law a Constitutional Convention for the purpose of amending the U.S. Constitution in the following respects strictly according to the rules of procedure specified below.

1. **Rules of Procedure.** The Constitutional Convention shall be conducted according to the following rules.

1.1 Robert's Rules of Order shall apply except the Convention may adopt such other rules and conveniences as were used by the Constitutional Convention of 1787.

1.2 No amendment or additions to the amendments set forth in Section 2 hereof shall be made unless germane to the amendments set forth in Section 2. An objection to germaneness shall be by point of order and shall be ruled on by the Chair. The standards of germaneness shall include the following:

   (a) No proposed amendment to the Constitution shall seek to amend any provision of the Constitution not the subject of an amendment identified herein.

   (b) All amendments to the proposed amendments herein shall relate to the subject matter of the proposed amendments.

   (c) A specific proposed amendment may not be amended by an amendment general in nature.

   (d) A general proposed amendment may be amended by an amendment specific in nature.

1.3 The Convention shall not make any amendment, addition, or change to any part of the U.S. Constitution not germane to the amendments set forth in Section 2, nor shall it amend, add to, or change, directly or indirectly, any portion of the U.S. Constitution not specified below for amendment, nor shall it amend, add to, or change directly or indirectly, any portion of the Bill of Rights except to clarify the Tenth Amendment to restore powers intended to be in the States by the Founding Fathers. Any violation of the foregoing prohibitions shall exceed the authority of the Convention and shall be void without affecting the balance of the actions taken.

2. **Proposed Amendments.** The Constitution shall be amended as follows:

28th Amendment. The following shall replace the second paragraph of Section 7 of Article I of the Constitution:

Every bill not an appropriation bill which shall have passed the House of Representatives and the Senate shall, before it becomes a law, be presented to the President of the United States. If he approves, he shall sign it, but if not, he shall return it with his objections to the House in which it shall have originated, which shall enter the objections at large in its journal and proceed to reconsider it. If after such reconsideration two-thirds of that House shall agree to pass the bill, it shall be sent, together with the objections, to the other House, by which it shall likewise be reconsidered, and if approved by two-thirds of that House, it shall become a law. Every appropriation bill which shall have passed the House of Representatives and the Senate shall, before it becomes law, be presented to the President of the United States; if he approves, he shall sign it, but if he approves it in part, he shall sign it as to the sections approved and shall return the bill with the parts not approved with his objections to that House in which it shall have originated, which shall thereupon proceed in the manner provided for above with respect to bills which are not appropriation bills. If the parts objected to are not approved as there provided, such parts shall not be law, but the parts approved shall be law.

29th Amendment. The following seven paragraphs shall be added to Section 9 of Article I of the Constitution:

No member of any committee of Congress shall serve on such a committee for longer than four terms in the House and two terms in the Senate as those terms are defined in Sections 1 and 2 of Article I of the Constitution.

Any existing law in conflict with the Twenty-Ninth Amendment shall be void except any law in conflict with Clause 10 of the Thirtieth Amendment shall not be void until two years after its adoption, during which time Congress shall extinguish all prohibited benefits and pay or promise to pay the present value thereof determined actuarially using a discount rate of 10 percent per annum, as of the date of such adoption, to those whose benefits are terminated thereby, with any deferred payment made without interest on such terms and conditions and over such time as Congress shall establish.

Direct and indirect compensation for members of Congress shall be equal. Compensation for members of Congress and their staff shall be established every four years beginning on the first day of the second calendar year following the effective date of the adoption of this amendment by a majority vote of a committee of six, two appointed by Congress, two by the President, and two by a majority vote of the governors of the several States, one each for a term of two years and one each for a term of four years with appointments made in like manner every two years for a term of four years. Committee deadlocks lasting more than thirty days shall be resolved by the President upon application of any committee member. Such committee shall have the power to appropriate from the federal treasury such funds as shall be required to perform its duties, including the compensation and expenses of the members thereof, which shall be of public record and never exceed for a committee member the amount established for a member of Congress proportionally reduced to his time of actual service. Appropriations to cover all other costs of operating Congress are reserved to Congress.

All bills and each and every provision thereof or amendment thereto shall be passed by Congress as provided in the Constitution by votes, and all votes shall be public, be recorded, and be published by voter.

One-third of the members of each House shall have the right to have a vote by their House on any bill whether in committee or not.

Both Houses shall agree on a budget for the succeeding year no later than October 1 of the prior year, failing which none of the members thereof shall be qualified to hold elective office in Congress after the expiration of his or her then existing term of office. All future budgets shall be compared to the current year's budget on both a cash and accrual basis, and such comparison shall be part of the budget.

No emergency appropriation bill whose purpose is to prevent or mitigate or respond to a loss of life or property or a threat to national security shall be valid if it contains any non-emergency spending authorization.

30ᵗʰAmendment. The following eleven changes shall be included in a new Section 11 to be added to Article I of the Constitution:

Congress shall have no power to pass any bill for raising revenue or for appropriating money unless it is approved by three-fifths of both Houses;

To pass any retroactive bill unless approved by a two-thirds vote of both Houses except Congress shall never impose taxes retroactively.

To pass any bill using its power under the Sixteenth Amendment that is effective before the first day of the calendar year following its enactment without a two-thirds vote of both Houses and no such bill shall ever be made subject to a stated term.

After the adoption of this amendment, to impose an enforceable duty upon State, local, or tribal governments or entities by which they do business without their written consent or to discriminate against them in the provision of federal assistance, financial or otherwise, because they refuse to consent.

To pass any bill limiting the amount of contributions by any United States domiciliary corporation or organization or citizen to any corporation, organization, or person for political purposes involving federal policy or federal candidates nor limiting the expenditures of any of the foregoing as long as both the contributions and expenditures are fully and promptly disclosed to the public by the most public and technological means available for such purpose.

To pass any bill unless it sets forth at the beginning thereof a declaration of the purpose thereof and the constitutional power under which it is brought, a statement that the bill is needed in the public interest, a statement that the government can afford the bill, a statement that the government can administer the bill in a way people can respect, a statement of its impact on the freedoms of the citizens, and a statement of its possible unintended consequences.

To provide financial assistance to, or purchase any debt securities of, any State or entity by which it does business or subdivisions or municipalities thereof unless the financial assistance or purchase is provided to all States and prorated by population determined by the most recent census or unless approved by a two-thirds vote of both Houses.

To exempt itself from any law, or be separately classified so as to be treated differently from the people generally.

To appropriate monies for any year for which a budget has been established by Congress a sum greater than one-fifth of the Gross Domestic Product of the United States for the prior year as determined by Congress unless the appropriation is approved by a two-thirds vote of both Houses.

To pass any bill conferring a retirement, health, pension, or other benefit upon itself or its past, present, or future members or any employee of the United States or agency thereof, except the military, unless such bill applies generally to all other citizens.

To pass any bill delegating to the President the authority to take any action subject to Congress's disapproval or to increase spending authority related to any government obligations the budget authority for which has not been provided in advance, unless such delegation is necessary and accompanied by clearly defined and ascertainable standards.

31st Amendment. The following new paragraph shall be added at the end of the second paragraph of Section 2 of Article II of the Constitution:

The President shall nominate ambassadors, other public ministers and consuls, judges of the Supreme Court, and all other federal courts established by Congress upon the advice and consent of the Senate within ninety days of any vacancy, and the Senate shall confirm or reject such nomination within 120 days thereafter, whereupon, if the nomination is consented to, the President shall appoint the person so nominated within thirty days. If the President or the Senate, as the case may be, do not timely act, the compensation otherwise payable to the President or members of the Senate and its staff shall be abated without recoupment until such action is taken.

32nd Amendment. The following five paragraphs shall be included in a new Section 5 to be added to Article II of the Constitution:

All agencies of the federal government having the authority to issue regulations shall receive a priority number by the President by January 1 of each even-numbered year with the highest priority being the lowest number. Conflicts among valid regulations among agencies shall be resolved in favor of the agency having the highest priority. New agencies not having a priority number shall have the lowest priority in the order established unless the President amends his prior prioritization.

The delegation of legislative power by Congress to the President or any department or executive agency shall be accompanied by standards and shall be strictly construed. If there is any doubt concerning whether a government official has delegated power, the presumption shall be that he does not. Courts shall not defer to the judgment of legislative or executive officials with respect to their power nor accord to them any presumption of authority but shall require strict proof. Whether any regulation is authorized by law is at any trial a question of fact for the trier of fact, though the court can reverse a finding that authority exists if it believes as a matter of law there is no authority. No agency to which legislative power is delegated shall have any privilege to withhold information from Congress.

Except to correct mistakes in regulations that impose greater restrictions on the people than were intended, proposed regulations made by any agency of the United States shall have no effect for any purpose whatsoever until they are adopted, and then their effect shall be prospective.

No person shall be required to file an application to obtain a right or permit required by law with more than one agency or department, and that agency or department shall coordinate as it deems appropriate with other agencies and departments that have an interest in the matter. If more than one agency or department requires an application for permit, the applicant has the right to select which of the agencies or departments shall receive his application unless otherwise specified by law. Any such application shall be acted upon by the agency or department within one year from the filing thereof or shall thereafter be deemed unconditionally approved as filed. A denial, or approval with conditions that are not satisfied within six months from agency action from the applicant's submission of a satisfaction of conditions, shall be subject to judicial review before the federal court of appeals of the circuit in which the applicant resides.

Upon request of the House of Representatives, the President shall appear before it while in session to answer questions but not more often than weekly and for not more than forty minutes for each appearance.

33rd Amendment. The following two paragraphs shall be added to Article V of the Constitution:

Whenever a majority of the legislatures of the several States propose amendments to this Constitution, they shall file the same with Congress, which shall within four months return the proposed amendments to the legislatures of the several States with such advice as it deems appropriate and, upon such return or upon the failure of Congress to timely make such return, the proposed amendments, with Congress's return, if any, shall be submitted to the legislatures of the several States and, when ratified by the legislatures of three-fourths of the several States, the proposed amendments shall be valid to all intents and purposes according to the provisions thereof.

Any amendment changing the Bill of Rights or the Thirteenth, Fourteenth, or Fifteenth Amendments shall not be valid unless ratified by all the States.

34th Amendment. The following five paragraphs shall be added to Article VI of the Constitution:

Notwithstanding Amendment XXIV, as long as the United States obtains revenue under the Sixteenth Amendment, every citizen of the United States eighteen years or older shall file an income tax return and, notwithstanding any other law or provision of this Constitution, make a tax payment equal to the cost of operating Congress divided by the last census of the population of the United States rounded to the nearest dollar but not more than the cost of one-fourth troy ounce of silver nor less than ten dollars and, upon payment, shall receive evidence thereof, which evidence shall be shown as a condition to the right of such person to vote in any federal election. Such amount until changed by Congress shall be ten dollars and, when changed by Congress, shall be published by the President no later than the first business day after January 1 of each even-numbered year.

The total size of all regulations issued by all agencies and departments of the United States, measured in bytes of text, shall not exceed four times those contained in all federal statutes, and any regulations in excess of such amount shall be void as of January 1 of each even-numbered year in the reverse order of the promulgating agency's priority. No later than November 1 of each odd-numbered year, Congress shall publish the bytes of text in all federal statutes effective for the following year, and the President shall publish the bytes of text in all regulations of all agencies by priority number for the following year.

Regulations shall be void ten years after they are effective unless earlier approved by Congress for a stated term. Congress shall have the authority to exempt specified regulations from this provision.

Unless increased by a majority vote of the State legislatures upon the request of Congress, the total staff answerable to each member of the House of Representatives and Senate and their committees shall not exceed twenty-five thousand persons for allocation among them as the members of Congress deem appropriate.

No person in government, elected, hired, or appointed, shall suppress any information relating to the sighting or existence of extraterrestrial phenomena and shall have a duty to preserve and disclose any such information to the public promptly as it becomes available, including information existing at the time of the adoption of this amendment.

35ᵗʰ Amendment. The Tenth Amendment to the Constitution is amended to read as follows:

Section 1. The powers not delegated to the United States by the Constitution, nor prohibited by it to the States, are reserved to the States respectively, or to the people. Such powers shall include all those powers not expressly delegated to Congress under the Constitution, whether or not those powers existed prior to the adoption of the Constitution or those arising thereafter as a result of the Constitution. The States shall not exercise these powers in a way that diminishes or interferes with the powers expressly delegated by the Constitution to Congress, the President, or the Judiciary.

Section 2. The legislature of each State shall have the power to limit the terms of the senators and representatives in Congress representing such State.

Section 3. The legislatures of two-thirds of the several States shall have the power to repeal any law or part thereof or regulation of the United States or remove any federal judge or justice of the Supreme Court by a resolution describing the law or part thereof or regulation to be repealed or judge or justice to be removed with the effective date of such action being as stated in the resolution or upon obtaining the required approval, whichever date is later. Upon the required approval, the resolution shall be signed by the governors of the States having the approving legislatures, shall contain a certification of approval, and shall be delivered to the President and Congress by the governor last to sign and shall take effect as provided therein.

Section 4. There is hereby established a Board of Governors whose members shall be the governors of the several States, which shall act according to rules adopted by the governors of the several States. The Board of Governors shall have power by a two-thirds vote of its members to make recommendations to Congress or to their State legislatures and to administer all activities assigned to the States or State legislatures herein as they deem in the best interests of the United States. The Board of Governors shall be immune from all taxes.

Section 5. Any approval by the legislatures of the States as used in the Constitution means approval by a majority of all members of each House in their legislative branch.

36th Amendment. The following Thirty-Sixth Amendment shall be added to the Constitution:

Section 1. Whether any law or regulation is unconstitutional as applied to particular circumstances is a question of fact for the trier of fact, though the court can reverse a finding by a jury of constitutionality as applied if it believes the law is unconstitutional as applied.

Section 2. Every citizen shall have standing in court to seek a declaration of the meaning of any part of the Constitution or to challenge the constitutionality or validity of any federal law or regulation or to seek the meaning thereof.

Section 3. No person shall be guilty of a federal crime unless the person's mens rea has been proved beyond a reasonable doubt.

Section 4. If any part of a bill that becomes law is determined to be unconstitutional, the whole law shall be unconstitutional.

Section 5. The Seventeenth Amendment to the Constitution is repealed.

Section 6. The "general Welfare" as used in the Preamble of the Constitution refers to the whole of the American people and does not grant Congress any power with respect to any class of people. Congress shall have no discretionary power to spend money in aid of the "general Welfare" as used in Article I § 8 cl. 1 of the Constitution pursuant to a power not expressly enumerated in the Constitution, unless its action is approved by a two-thirds vote of both Houses.

Section 7. Doubts as to whether the President can lawfully assert executive privilege on any matter to avoid releasing information to Congress shall be resolved against the President.

3. **Clearing Agent.** The governor of the State of _____ _____ is appointed as a clearing agent for the States to receive and submit to Congress action taken by the States hereunder as provided below or as otherwise implied and incidental to the purposes of this Resolution.

4. **Ratification Procedures.** The preceding proposed amendments to the Constitution shall be laid before the legislatures of each of the several States. When a State adopts a resolution consenting to this Constitutional Convention Resolution, it shall submit such approval, duly authenticated, to the Governor of the State of _____. Each State legislature shall consent to Sections 1, 3, and 4 of this Constitutional Convention Resolution and shall consent to such of the proposed amendments in Section 2 as it deems appropriate.

Each proposed amendment herein shall be separately approved by each State legislature as it deems appropriate before _____, 20___. The failure to approve by such date shall be treated as non-approval.

When the governor of the State of _____ has received resolutions from two-thirds of the several States (currently thirty-four States) consenting to this Constitutional Convention Resolution as provided, such governor shall submit the same, together with proof of the approvals of the legislatures of two-thirds of the several States, to the United States Congress, and, upon such submission, the Constitutional Convention Resolution shall constitute an application under Article V of the Constitution, which shall require the Congress to proceed according to the provisions thereof.

Congress is requested to adopt the proposed amendments to the Constitution without change as its own and promptly to submit them to the States for ratification, failing which it shall call a

Convention for approving the amendments. Congress is further requested to specify in such a call whether the ratification of amendments forthcoming from the Convention shall be ratified by three-fourths of the State legislature or conventions in the States. When one or more of the amendments are ratified by legislatures of three-fourths of the several States, they shall be valid to all intents and purposes, as part of the Constitution, even though other proposed amendments are not ratified or are pending ratification.

E

CURRICULUM VITAE OF JOHN M. COGSWELL

JOHN M. COGSWELL
415 E. Main Street
Buena Vista, CO 81211

BORN:

August 17, 1939, in Del Norte, Colorado. Raised on ranches in Saguache, Colorado, and western Kansas.

EDUCATION:

St. Andrew's School, Middletown, Delaware (Cum Laude), 1957, President of Senior Class and Student Body, Captain of Wrestling Team.

Yale University, New Haven, Connecticut, B.A. History, 1961, Captain of Heavyweight Crew.

Georgetown Law Center, Washington, DC, LLB (6th out of 120), worked for Congressman Bob Dole for three years full-time while attending law school full-time.

Basic School, USMC, February 1965 (3rd out of 250).

Naval Justice School, USN, 1965 (2nd out of 78).

MILITARY:

U.S. Marine Corps. Released from active service as a captain in August 1967.

PROFESSIONAL:

In the U.S. Marine Corp., between 1965 and 1967, Mr. Cogswell handled approximately seventy-five special and general courts-martial, trial and defense. After three years of oil and gas practice with a small firm, Mr. Cogswell started his own firm in 1970, which grew to forty-four lawyers in 1987. This firm disintegrated during the economic downturn in Denver in the late 1980s.

Currently, Mr. Cogswell has a law office in Buena Vista, Colorado. He has been admitted to the bars of the U.S. Supreme Court, U.S. Court of Appeals for the 10th Circuit, U.S. Court of Appeals for the District of Columbia, U.S. District Courts in Colorado, Kansas, and the District of Columbia, U.S. Court of Military Appeals, U.S. Tax Court, and the Supreme Courts of Colorado and Kansas. He has been practicing law for forty-eight years.

Mr. Cogswell's practice emphasizes complex commercial litigation and business and commercial transactions. He has been lead counsel in major class action cases representing sugar beet growers and oil and gas royalty and small share working interest owners producing CO_2 gas. He has been involved in numerous other cases, agriculturally related and otherwise, in State and federal courts, both trial and appellate. He has had an "AV" rating from Martindale-Hubbell since the early 1970s.

OTHER:

Candidate for the U.S. Senate in 1978 and 1980. Arapahoe County GOP Chairman, 1981–1983; prior director and trustee of various nonprofit institutions; director and secretary of Colorado Wildlife Heritage Foundation; and, between 1989 and 1998, General Partner of T-Bar Ranch, Ltd., which owned and operated a 1,200-head cow ranch near Goodland, Kansas.

NOTES

1. Woodruff, Paul. *Reverence: Renewing a Forgotten Virtue.* New York: Oxford University Press, 2001, p. 56.

2. Solzhenitsyn, Alexander. *One Day in the Life of Ivan Denisovich.* New York: E.P. Dutton & Co., 1991, p. 69.

3. Hamilton, Alexander. "Federalist No. 15" in *The Federalist Papers.* New York: Signet Classic, an imprint of New American Library, a division of Penguin Putnam, Inc. 1961, pp. 110–111.

4. Machiavelli, Niccolo. *The Prince and the Discourses.* New York: Random House, 1950.

5. Bradford, Ernle D. S. *The Great Siege: Malta 1565.* Chatham, Kent, Great Britain: Wordsworth Editions Limited, 1961, p. 195.

6. Ibid., p. 195.

7. Ibid., pp. 198–199.

8. Hook, Sidney. *The Hero in History.* New Brunswick, New Jersey: Transaction publishers, 1992, p. 151.

9. Ibid., p. 151.

10. Plato. *Protagoras.* 322 c.

11. Madison, James. "Federalist No. 10" in *The Federalist Papers.* New York: Signet Classic, an imprint of New American Library, a division of Penguin Putnam, Inc. 1961, p. 77.

12. Woodruff, Paul. *First Democracy.* New York: Oxford University Press, 2005, p. 15.

13. Madison, James. "Federalist No. 57" in *The Federalist Papers.* New York: Signet Classic, an imprint of New American Library, a division of Penguin Putnam, Inc. 1961, p. 97.

14. Editorial. "Filibustering Nominees Must End." The New York Times. January 28, 2012. The New York Times Sunday Review, The Opinion Pages. <http://www.nytimes.com/2012/01/29/opinion/sunday/filibustering-nominees-must-end.html>.

15. Chatelain, Maurice. *Our Cosmic Ancestors*. Sedona, Arizona: Temple Golden Publications, 1987, pp. 27–28.

16. Burney, Nathaniel. "Too Many Federal Crimes, Too Many without *Mens Rea*—Do We Have a Movement Yet?" The Criminal Lawyer. September 28, 2011. <http://www.burneylawfirm.com/blog/category/statutes/>.

17. Hall, Jerome (quoting Professor Francis Bowes *Sayre, Mens Rea, 45 Harv. L. Rev. 974 (1932)*, quoting Oliver Wendell Holmes). *General Principles of Criminal Law*. Clark, New Jersey: THE LAWBOOK EXCHANGE, LTD., 2005, p. 74.

18. Madison, James. "Federalist No. 55" in *The Federalist Papers*. New York: Signet Classic, an imprint of New American Library, a division of Penguin Putnam, Inc. 1961, p. 342.

19. Hamilton, Alexander. "Federalist No. 1" in *The Federalist Papers*. New York: Signet Classic, an imprint of New American Library, a division of Penguin Putnam, Inc. 1961, p. 33.

20. Hayek, F. A. *Law, Legislature and Liberty, Vol. 2., The Mirage of Social Justice*. Chicago: The University of Chicago Press, 1976, p. 3.

21. Murray, William Hutchison. *The Scottish Himalayan Expedition*. Indiana: Indiana University, Dent, 1951.

22. Hayek, F. A. *The Constitution of Liberty*. Chicago: The University of Chicago Press, 1960, pp. 54, 62, 67, 68.

23. Hayek, F. A. *The Fatal Conceit*. Chicago: The University of Chicago Press, 1988, pp. 34, 35.

24. Woodruff, Paul. *First Democracy,* p. 67.

25. Ibid., p. 63.

26. Ibid., p. 69.

27. Grossman, Vasily. *Forever Flowing*. Evanston, Ill: Northwestern University Press, 1997, pp. 99, 194.

28. Cogswell, John. *Voice of the Plains*. Castro Valley, California: Greenridge Press, 1987, p. 61.

29. Hook, Sidney. *The Hero in History*, pp. 24, 25.

30. Woodruff, Paul. *First Democracy,* p. 154.

31. Ibid., p. 6.

32. Ibid., p. 6.

33. Frankl, Viktor E. *Man's Search for Meaning*. Boston, Massachusetts: Beacon Press, 1959.

34. Pope John XXIII. "Mater et Magistra; Encylcical of Pope John XXIII on Christianity and Social Progress." The Vatican, The Holy See. May 15, 1961. <http://www.vatican.va/holy_father/john_xxiii/encyclicals/documents/hf_j-xxiii_enc_15051961_mater_en.html>.

35. Hayek, F. A. *The Constitution of Liberty*.

36. Tetlock, Philip E., Ph.D. *Expert Political Judgment: How Good Is It? How Can We Know?* New Jersey: Princeton University Press, 2005.

37. Drucker, P. F. *The Unseen Revolution: How Pension Fund Socialism Came to America*. New York: Harper & Row, 1976.

38. Durant, Will and Ariel. *The Lessons of History*. New York: Simon and Schuster, 1968, p. 77.

39. Hook, Sidney. *The Hero in History*, pp. 24, 25.

40. Cicero. *The Republic*. Cambridge, Massachusetts: Harvard University Press, Loeb's Classical Library ed., 2006.

41. Ibid.

42. Hamilton, Alexander. "Federalist No. 33" in *The Federalist Papers*. New York: Signet Classic, an imprint of New American Library, a division of Penguin Putnam, Inc. 1961, p. 201.

43. Krause, Sharon. *Liberalism With Honor*. Cambridge, Massachusetts: Harvard University Press, 2002. p. 190.

44. Woodruff, Paul. *Reverence: Renewing a Forgotten Virtue*, pp. 165–166.

45. Machiavelli, Niccolo. *The Prince and the Discourses*.

46. von Mises, Ludwig. *Liberalism in the Classical Tradition*. Indianapolis: Liberty Fund, 2005, pp. 12–14.

47. Epstein, Richard. "Does U.S. Economic Inequality Have a Good Side?" PBS NewsHour. October 26, 2011. <http://www.pbs.org/newshour/bb/business/july-dec11/makingsense_10-26.html>.

48. Gordon, Robert J. "Misperceptions About the Magnitude and Timing of Changes in American Income Inequality National Bureau of Economic Research." The National Bureau of Economic Research. September, 2009. <http://www.nber.org/papers/w15351>.

49. Wilson, James Q. "Angry About Inequality? Don't Blame the Rich." *The Washington Post-Opinions*. January 26, 2012.

50. Ridley, Matt. *The Origins of Virtue* Great Britain: Penguin Books Ltd., 1996, p. 262.

51. Ibid., p. 265.

52. Ibid.

53. Ortega y Gasset, Jose. *The Revolt of the Masses.* New York: W. W. Norton & Company, Inc., 1932, p. 113.

54. Ibid.

55. Wapshott, Nicholas (quoting John Maynard Keynes). *Keynes Hayek: The Clash That Defined Modern Economics.* W. W. Norton & Company, 2011.

56. Hamilton, Alexander. "Federalist No. 1" in *The Federalist Papers.* New York: Signet Classic, an imprint of New American Library, a division of Penguin Putnam, Inc. 1961, p. 33.

57. Sacks, Jonathan, Rabbi. *The Dignity of Difference: How to Avoid the Clash of Civilizations.* London; New York: Continuum Books, 2002, p. 84.

58. Woodruff, Paul. *First Democracy,* p. 81.

59. Washington, George. "George Washington's Farewell Address to the People of the United States." United States Government Printing Office. 106th Congress 2nd Session Senate Document 106-21, Washington, 2000. <http://www.gpo.gov/fdsys/pkg/GPO-CDOC-106sdoc21/pdf/GPO-CDOC-106sdoc21.pdf>.

INDEX

A

accountability, 33, 42, 91, 111, 122, 130

action: arbitrary, 117; as core value of American culture, 148–149; drivers for political action, 170; governmental, 117–118; individual, 151; necessity of, 171; as social insurance, 167

action plan (Campaign Constitution), 242–244

actual harm, 124

Adams, John, 82

adversary debates, 157, 162

advertisements, voters and, 54

"Advice and Consent," 69

Advisory Committee (Campaign Constitution), 6–7, 8, 239, 242

Aesop, 153

Affordable Care Act, 94, 128, 186–187

agencies. *See* federal agencies

agreements on methods, 147–148

Air Force regulations, 72

Aldrin, Edwin, 104

aliens (extraterrestrials), 19, 102–105, 218, 258

aliens (immigrants), 143

Allen v. Wright, 120

ambition, 140, 187

ambitions, 40

amendments. *See also* proposed amendments: Campaign Constitution's support, 241; Constitutional Conventions, 3–5; Constitutional process for, 240–241; emergency bills, 39; future amendments, 244–245; process amendments, 237–239; proposed, summary of, 15–21; ratification procedures, 261–262; state amendments, 18, 85–87, 216, 257

American culture: as engine of production, xviii–xix; principles for, 147–149

American Indians, 189

ancient Greek society: good judgment in, 157; loss of democracy, 187; lottery method, 174; money in politics and, 53; notions of freedom and, 152–153; protection against wealthy, 174; reasons for downfall, 139; speaking in assembly, 153; today's government resembling, 188

annual budgets: approval process, 37–38; timely, 16, 37–38, 206, 253; tying to GDP, 61–62

Apollo program, 103–104

applications, multiple, to agencies, 79–81

appointments, timely, 17, 69–71, 211, 255

"appropriate" activities, 121

appropriations: emergency bills, 16, 39, 206, 253; limits on, 61–62; line-item vetoes, 15, 23–24, 201, 251; super majority for, 16, 40–42, 207, 253

arbitrary government actions, 20, 116–118, 260

Armstrong, Neil, 104

Army regulations, 72

articles of Constitution. *See under* Constitution; proposed amendments

astronauts, 103

Athenians. *See* ancient Greek society

Automobile Club of Michigan v. Commissioner, 48, 78

269

Give the Gift of

Fix the System
Reform the Constitution

to Your Friends and Colleagues

CHECK YOUR LEADING BOOKSTORE, ORDER HERE,

OR ORDER ONLINE AT

www.campaignconstitution.com

❑ **YES**, I want _____ copies of *Fix the System: Reform the Constitution* at $14.95 each, plus $4.95 shipping per book (Colorado residents please add $.43 sales tax per book). Canadian orders must be accompanied by a postal money order in U.S. funds. Allow 15 days for delivery.

❑ **YES**, I am interested in having John M. Cogswell speak or give a seminar to my company, association, school, or organization. Please send information.

My check or money order for $_____ is enclosed.

Please charge my: ❑ Visa   ❑ MasterCard

                               ❑ Discover   ❑ American Express

Name_____

Organization _____

Address _____

City/State/Zip _____

Phone_____ Email _____

Card # _____

Security Code: _____Exp. Date_____ Signature_____

Please make your check payable and return to:
CAMPAIGN CONSTITUTION PRESS
PO Box 1430, 15099 County Road 350 • Buena Vista, CO 81211

JOHN M. COGSWELL
AUTHOR STATEMENT

John M. Cogswell, a fifth generation Coloradoan and practicing lawyer for 48 years, believes the method of federal government decision-making which has evolved under the Constitution has given us leaders who have diminished our unalienable rights of "Life, Liberty and the Pursuit of Happiness" as envisioned by the Founding Fathers.

He argues that the only way to recover this vision is to change the character of our leaders by changing the way decisions are made. To do this, he recommends process amendments to the Constitution initiated by the States under their Article V power because Congress, which has the most to lose by needed changes, will never fix the system.

In furtherance of his recommendations, he has proposed 44 amendments to the Constitution and written a short commentary on each of them and other essays for public discussion. He has also outlined a method for realizing these changes under the leadership of Campaign Constitution, a nonprofit corporation, whose business plan details necessary action.

Those who share his view will find a workable method for reforming the Constitution with changes needed to recapture the spirit of freedom and limited government underlying the foundation of America. Whether this happens is up to you – whether you will don the spirit of Paul Revere and spread "the alarm through every Middlesex village and farm". Our future depends on it. The mission is clear. The window is narrow. The time is short. Our freedoms are at risk.